Mommy, Teach Me to Read!

Mommy, Teach Me to Read!

A Complete and Easy-to-Use Home Reading Program

Barbara Curtis

B&H
PUBLISHING GROUP

Nashville, Tennessee

ISBN: 978-0-8054-4477-3

Published by B&H Publishing Group
Nashville, Tennessee

Dewey Decimal Classification: 372.4
Subject Heading: READING \ HOME SCHOOLING

Unless otherwise noted, Scripture quotations are from the Holy Bible, New
International Version, copyright © 1973, 1978, 1984 by International Bible
Society. Other version includes KJV, The King James Version.

5 6 7 8 9 10   19 18 17 16 15

For every mommy
busy building our cultural heritage
one story at a time.

Table of Contents

Acknowledgments

ONE OF THE GREATEST ACCOMPLISHMENTS OF my life has been teaching children to read, as well as teaching parents to teach their children to read.

I am so grateful to the Washington Montessori Institute—where I received my training—for equipping me with a simple and effective approach to reading that worked so well for me as a teacher.

But what I never could have guessed back then was how beautifully it would work when I taught my own children to read at home. Half of my twelve are grown-ups now, but I treasure memories of them curled up with books, choosing wisely and eager to discuss what they were reading. I'm glad they love to read, but I'm doubly grateful to have been part of launching such an important and rewarding part of their lives.

I'm also grateful to B&H Publishing Group for this opportunity to share the things I learned as a teacher and applied as a mom—thus equipping even more parents with the tools they need to give their children a successful start in reading and to discover that same sense of accomplishment and joy.

A special thank-you to my editor, Zan Tyler, for promoting this project and trusting me to deliver. And thanks to my wonderful and supportive family for sharing Mommy for a little while.

Barbara

Waterford, Virginia
September 2006

Introduction

THIS BOOK IS INTENDED AS A companion volume to follow *Mommy, Teach Me!* while the first book presents an easy-to-use preschool curriculum in all other areas, language is what you will find here in the pages of *Mommy, Teach Me to Read!*—a parent-friendly approach to speech and reading development from birth to seven. You will also discover a preschool approach to history and singing, since these are language-intensive subjects.

Mommy, Teach Me to Read! is based on my second book *Ready, Set, Read!* first published in 1997. The content has been updated and expanded because— well, frankly because I've been continuously updated and expanded! Expanded not only through ten more years of mothering, but through ten years of using the Internet as a communications tool. My blog www.MommyLife.net has for the past several years kept me in close contact with mothers of preschoolers, whose questions have stimulated and challenged me, adding to what I have to share through my books.

The Internet is a blessing for all of us who are looking for ways to help our children reach their potential and allowing God to help us reach our own. With a multitude of resources available, part of the help I want to offer you moms is to search out the best so your time will not be wasted with your computer instead of your kids. The minute my book titles were secure, I purchased the domain name www.MommyTeachMe.net. Anyone who reads either of the *Mommy, Teach Me!* books will also have access to a dynamic and jam-packed resource, offering links to teaching supplies and online support. A real bonus is the templates for materials such as sandpaper letters, phonetic flash cards, and other language exercises you will find described in these pages. For mothers who are more often than not Lone-Rangering it with young children, this will be an important support as you begin to make the most of your child's preschool years, the years when it is truly easiest to teach children to read.

Throughout the text, when you see the icon 🍎, that is your signal that there are more resources, information, or support at the Web site. Keep in mind that the information flow there is two-way, so if you come across resources you think should be included, I'm only an e-mail away.

Please know that I am not the kind of "expert" who thinks my way is God's way. I simply share what I was taught and what worked for me. If you don't have the time or energy to make use of every single idea presented in this book, that is not cause for discouragement. Just do what works for you, feeling free to modify and combine with bits and pieces you pick up elsewhere.

One other small but important note for readers: I'm asking my readers to please understand my use of the word *he* in the very old-fashioned way it was intended—as a pronoun covering all individuals without regard to gender. It is not a slight on women or daughters—after all, I am one and have four of my own. I just want to focus on the task at hand and not be stumbling over words.

Now, let's begin!

Reading—the Great Adventure

YOU CAN DO IT! YOU CAN teach your children to read. You can open the gateway to a rich, rewarding adventure that will beckon them on for the rest of their lives. You can set their feet on the path to a lifelong love of reading.

Through teaching your children yourself, in an informal and loving way, you can control the momentum, drawing each child closer to reading at a pace tailored to his own individual needs. You can anticipate your children's trouble spots and give them extra encouragement when they need it, thus diverting feelings of inadequacy or failure, which make for unmotivated readers later on.

Your investment will build in each of your children eagerness and self-confidence—making every realm of knowledge as available as an open book. In addition, your involvement in their first efforts will nurture a love of words and ideas that will boost your children's potential for success—no matter where their future finds them.

Teaching your child to read may sound like a tall order for an ordinary parent. It isn't. Since the first hieroglyphics, most children who learned to read learned to read at home, taught by their parents. This resulted in some charming and intimate teaching methods, as when Hebrew parents baked cakes in the form of letters of the Hebrew alphabet, requiring their children to name the letters before they ate the cakes. Parents wrote words with honey for the child to read and lick from a slate, that "the words of the law might be sweet on his lips."

Reading was not a compartmentalized task that one had to leave the home to learn, but part of the family bond—parents and older siblings passing on the keys that would unlock the secrets of the books the children had been hearing read aloud for as long as they could remember. Reading was part of a natural flow in the development of the child.

In the United States, two factors brought about a change:

- the advent of public education, originally intended to extend literacy to every child, and

- our modern emphasis on specialization and the resulting public perception that learning occurs only in a certain building between specific hours by designated teachers.

Both these factors have eroded parents' confidence in their ability to teach their children anything—particularly reading skills. For decades we have left the most important part of our children's education to the "professionals," giving them credit for being better equipped to teach reading than we are.

But are they?

Consider the current state of affairs:

- According to the ACT (formerly American College Testing), only half of the 1.2 million high school seniors who took the 2005 test were prepared for the reading requirements of a first-year college course.[1]

- Colleges today routinely offer remedial courses for incoming freshman who failed to master material formerly required to graduate from high school.

- In January 2006, the National Survey of America's College Students found only 40 percent of the nation's college seniors are able to distinguish fact from commentary in a newspaper editorial or to understand instruction manuals.

- In August 1996, President Clinton announced the America Reads Challenge and pledged 2.75 billion dollars to ensure that every child could read well and independently by the end of third grade—a dramatic mandate that leaves me wondering how it was that at one time almost everyone used to read in first grade.

- Numerous expensive reading programs sell like hotcakes to worried parents who sense their children just aren't where they should be in school.

It doesn't sound as though the "professionals" are really better equipped at all!

That's because in the past few decades, public education has turned the reading realm upside down. Educrats (a term for educators in policy-making rather than teaching positions) arbitrarily replaced a consistently successful teaching method with something more modern—the "whole language" approach to reading. Now we are reaping the negative rewards of this failed experiment.

Didn't anyone notice that the traditional approach was producing the desired results? Perhaps they should have remembered the maxim *If it works, don't fix it.*

Phonetics First

What worked in teaching reading was phonetics, plain and simple. Why? Because English, despite the variations we trip over and laugh about, is basically a phonetic language.

Of some 500,000 words in the dictionary, 85 percent are phonetic.

Of course there are exceptions. Think of *ough*. I come up with six ways to say it: *oo* in thr*ough*, *uff* in r*ough*, *off* in c*ough*, *au* in b*ough*t, *o* in th*ough*, *ow* in b*ough*. Obviously words like these are learned only by sight. Sight recognition is part of any reading program.

But sight-reading is a secondary approach, part of an arsenal professionals call *word attack skills*. Word attack skills are all the tools we give a child to master reading. Important as it is to conquer the exceptions in the English language, sight-reading does not adequately replace a phonetic approach to reading.

You see, if a child is only taught to know words by sight, it could take him a lifetime to master 425,000 words (85 percent of our language). But if he learns to read phonetically, he has the tool to master most words and the confidence to pick up the other tools when needed.

The foundation of any valuable reading program, then, must be phonetics. A child who learns to read phonetically inherits a wealth of material available to practice his reading skills (see chapter 3 for a list of early readers). As his confidence grows, his motivation increases. Memorizing sight words actually becomes easier.

Although the public school system has been slow to admit its error and return to the tried and true phonetic approach to reading, many others have caught on. And they're making a lot of money. The media is saturated with ads for programs like *Hooked on Phonics* and *The Phonics Game*. Many parents are recognizing that they need to take responsibility for something they used to take for granted as part of their children's away-from-home education.

You picked up *Mommy, Teach Me to Read!* because you're interested in your child's reading development. You want to teach him to read. Or perhaps you want to improve his pre-reading skills before he begins the formal part of his education—in public, private, or homeschool. Or maybe you just want an overview of the language process, the better to evaluate schools, curriculums, teaching approaches.

Don't invest another dollar in reading materials before you've finished reading this book. You may be very surprised at how simple it actually is to produce an excellent and enthusiastic reader.

The good news is: you don't need to spend hundreds of dollars.

But the best news of all is that you can find the enormous satisfaction of teaching your child the most important skill he'll ever learn. I wrote this book to put a simple, successful, and very affordable approach to reading in the hands of as many parents as possible.

I'm a parent myself—of twelve children. Perhaps it's the mother in me that accounts for my deep concern for the pressures and worries other parents face. My desire is to unburden, enlighten, and encourage parents in any way I can. Fortunately, I have some special experience that enables me to do so.

About Me

As a new mother in 1970, I came across a book by Maria Montessori, *The Absorbent Mind*. I was immediately fascinated, as I could see the truth in her observations about children. How could I doubt them when my own toddler Samantha was living proof?

Maria Montessori had a devotion to children I couldn't help but admire. She had an ability to see the world through the eyes of toddlers when the rest of the world seemed to be passing them by.

At the turn of the century, she became the first woman doctor in Italy. But her real life's mission was children. Her work with children labeled "retarded" (today called "developmentally delayed") led her to find ways to teach them reading and writing. She was so successful that these "retarded" children were soon outperforming their "normal" peers.

But what seemed miraculous to others was a source of great concern to her. If these disadvantaged children could do so well, what was keeping happy, healthy children on such a low level? Maria Montessori's great love for children and belief in their potential motivated her to construct an educational method that would meet their needs at appropriate times.

I wanted to learn that method, so I returned to college and eventually to the Washington Montessori Institute to become a teacher. In the decades since, I have taught in classrooms on both the East and West coasts, in the inner city and suburbia, as well as children of all ethnic groups and social strata.

And eventually I became a mother of many. Samantha is now grown with five children of her own, and my second daughter, Jasmine, has five as well. By a stroke of God's grace, though my life took some unusual twists and turns, I eventually became a Christian and realized my true calling. In addition to those two daughters, I eventually had ten more children—seven by birth and three by adoption.[2]

For anyone reading *Mommy, Teach Me to Read!*, I recommend my first book *Mommy, Teach Me!* as well. Based on my thirty-six years of motherhood and ten years of homeschooling, it will teach you how to encourage qualities that will prepare your child for any kind of learning: independence, concentration, a sense of order, self-control. *Mommy, Teach Me!* also outlines exercises that lead into pre-reading skills: eye-hand coordination, pincer grasp (for writing) and left-to-right sequencing.

As in *Mommy, Teach Me!*, my purpose in *Mommy, Teach Me to Read!* is

- to dispel the mystique of professionalism around teaching young children,

- to share knowledge of the child's God-given potential for learning,

- to help parents discover their own potential as teachers, and

- to empower parents to lay a foundation of joyful lifelong learning (in this book, more specifically, reading) on which their children can build—in public, private, or homeschool.

Why an Early Start?

All my years with children—as a teacher and a mother—have confirmed what I originally learned from my first dose of Montessori: that the first five years of a child's life involve a period of intense absorption and learning. God has built into each child the potential for seeking knowledge.

Look closely at children's activities and you will see a sense of purposefulness, working toward understanding and mastering their small worlds. Maria Montessori noticed that slum children, who had no toys of their own, found crumbs of bread on the ground to examine and play with. What a testimony to the child's relentless drive to explore and learn about his environment!

More and more experts are zeroing in on the toddler years. Shortly after I published my first book, *Small Beginnings*, in the spring of 1997, Oprah Winfrey devoted a show to the importance of the toddler years; *Newsweek* magazine published a special issue called *Your Child*, including articles such as "How to Build a Baby's Brain." There is a growing realization that the majority of learning takes place before children enter kindergarten. That's when the child's drive to learn is strongest.

God gives the child this drive to explore and learn. You see it clearly in the toddler years: *learning is what we are made for.* It is our drive to learn that causes us to seek to know more about God and the world he created for us. Watch any preschooler learning to peel carrots, write his name, or count his pennies—you will see a child completely engrossed, a child who isn't learning because he *has* to, but because he *wants* to, a child who loves to learn.

What happens then that produces older children who are bored and blasé, reluctant to learn? Many experts would say that these children probably began learning too late and therefore lost their potential love of learning.

Montessori's idea was that the child had sensitive periods for learning, times when areas of knowledge could be acquired effortlessly if the conditions are right. The right conditions include age-appropriate environmental cues plus loving parents or teachers who understand the child's needs and try to steer his course in the right direction.

When we wait too long to teach children certain skills, they learn with more difficulty and less joy. When we help our children learn the appropriate skills at the appropriate times, learning takes place without strain, it is enjoyable, and it leads to the desire to learn more—thus creating a lifelong love of learning.

I believe this is what God intended for our children.

What parent doesn't want each child to reach his potential? And what parent wouldn't choose to make the learning process as filled with joy and satisfaction as possible? To be good stewards of what God has given us, we parents need to know when is the best time for our children to learn and what tools we need to give them.

The Sensitive Period for Reading

The sensitive period for reading, according to Montessori and confirmed by my own teaching experience, is before the age of six. I know that some educators argue otherwise, but perhaps they have not been using a method tailored to match the needs of young children. Young children learn differently from elementary age children. Most young children who are taught in the sequence you will find in chapter 2 of this book will be reading before they begin their formal education—wherever that may be.

I say *most* young children because there are exceptions. Some children just seem to be born with different timetables. I've experienced this firsthand in my own home. After twenty-five years of teaching preschoolers to read, I had my toughest time with my daughter Sophia.

Sophia finally learned to read in December 1996 at the age of seven, though I had used the same approach with her since the age of three. A "normal" child in every way, she seemed to be running on a different clock in this one area. She also gained confidence from learning sight words before the phonetic approach clicked with her. I think God wanted me to see—before I began teaching parents to teach reading—what a wide range of variation he has allowed.

I must admit there were times when I was almost ready to give up on Sophia. If you find yourself in this position, don't give up. Once Sophia began just barely sounding out three-letter phonetic words, she was so happy with her new ability that she kept pushing herself. Within six months she was reading at second-grade level and regaling her family with riddles from *Clubhouse Jr.* magazine (see appendix A). Today at sixteen, Sophia's favorite activity is reading, and her favorite author is Jane Austen, whose books she has read several times over.

All by way of saying, an approach is just that: an approach. It's not a straitjacket. And a child's lack of immediate success should never lead to his feeling like a failure. Nor to yours. Always encourage your child, keep trying, keep praying, and keep your sense of humor.

Also, try not to judge your own efforts in terms of failure and success. Learning is a process; it takes as long as it takes. See appendix B for my list of favorite encouraging words.

How I See It

Most reading programs offer techniques for teaching reading as though it were a stand-alone skill, like sewing or carpentry. But reading does not stand alone. It has deep roots. Reading is a natural extension of our human desire to communicate, which begins when baby first babbles. On an individual level, the drive to communicate shapes and is shaped by the child's unique personality, ever expanding his ability to understand, express, evaluate, and form his own ideas.

The ability to read is in many ways dependent on the child's early experience of language. Evidence continues to accumulate of a direct relationship between early environments rich in language and higher IQs.

When fifty-something Mortimer Zuckerman, editor-in-chief of *U.S. News and World Report*, had his first child in 1997, he devoted an entire back-page editorial to his concern for his daughter's future—rethinking the popular wisdom that quality time makes up for quantity time. Since recent studies indicate that most connections in the child's brain are laid down before the age of three, and since so much of that connecting is based on exposure to the spoken word, Zuckerman urged his readers to rethink their positions on day care. He came as close as he could to evangelizing for stay-at-home moms (or dads)—someone to talk to the baby all day.

I agree with Zuckerman. In general, babies at home do get a head start in language. And babies who have a head start in language will have a head start in reading as well. Because I believe reading is best understood in the context of our whole language development, this book will begin at birth.

My hope is to inspire a greater appreciation for the miracle of language, to add a spiritual dimension as you teach your children to read.

The Spiritual Aspect of Language

Language is a special gift from God. The first job God gave Adam was to name the animals. The ability to name and understand the things of our world is a distinctly human ability. Language allows us to share information, ideas, and feelings, enriching our relationships with others and with God.

The desire to communicate is obvious from the child's earliest months. Most children learn to speak without direct teaching. As long as everything in the environment is in order and the child is developmentally sound, he will pass certain milestones with no special effort on the parents' part. In chapter 1, we will discuss how children develop spoken language—from the first babbles to first words to first simple sentences.

This information can be of enormous benefit to you when you want to get your child off to a good start. As parents, the more we understand God's part in every aspect of our children's development, the more inspiration we will have to do our best. Partnering with God to release your child's potential is much easier than doing it alone. Through understanding God's design for your child's spoken language, you will be able to see how reading flows naturally from that. You will be better equipped and more confident in teaching your child to read.

In chapters 2 and 3 I will share a tried-and-true method of teaching children to read—using snatches of time and simple materials—in a way that fits in with everyday living.

Isn't this the way you want your child to feel about reading? Something warm and comfortable, part of his daily routine, not something reserved for a certain environment or for meeting specific assignments.

Chapter 4 will focus on how to lay a foundation for your child's future understanding of grammar and structure. If learning about the eight parts of speech sounds a little complex for preschoolers, keep in mind that we must take the natural intellectual development of the child into consideration. Children under eight are not abstract thinkers. Yet any concrete representations we present to them at this age will form a foundation on which later abstract principles can be built and understood. Although the word *preposition* is meaningless to a young child, the role it plays in our daily speech can be represented through playful activities—using, for instance, a play barn and a small plastic horse:

"The horse is in the barn."

"The horse is outside the barn."

"The horse is beside the fence."

"The horse jumps over the fence."

So once your child is reading—or even before—you can be laying the groundwork for his future understanding of what makes our language work. While this may seem a little esoteric, it is something that will give him an edge in the future, leading to better understanding of what he reads as well as clearer communication.

Each chapter will also offer insights into choosing books for the child at each particular level—from board books to picture books and read-aloud stories to the child's first readers and then to chapter books. A child at each stage has certain needs, certain emotional concerns, and books are a way of meeting them.

In addition, books can be a bridge to great ideas and solid values. The best children's books have a subtext—a message behind the story—that communicates something in addition to the story itself. Just as Jesus used parables to teach the people of his time, authors use children's stories to teach children. Parents need to be aware of this in order to make sure that what they are reading enhances the values they are building at home. There is much too much good stuff out there to waste time with anything second rate!

Let's Get Started

I'm a firm believer in this: the best teachers love what they're doing. I've enjoyed teaching reading because I love to read myself. As a child, I preferred reading to almost any other activity. As an adult, I find books are my number one interest—after my family.

If that's the case with you, you're already off to a great start. If not, I'd like to suggest that you try to find a new interest or rekindle an old one in reading. If you never developed a love for books, it's never too late to give them another try.

You may find a different experience when you choose to read a classic that you thought you hated when it was forced on you. One of my most rewarding experiences has been reading *David Copperfield* aloud to my children. My husband, Tripp, has read many classics to our children, night after night, chapter by chapter. As a result, their memories, vocabularies, and empathy for others have grown.

Remember, children learn best by example. That can be a powerful motivation for us to change when we see that by changing we can offer our children so much more. God blesses our commitment to change for the sake of our children; sometimes he even makes it seem easy.

One of the wonderful gifts God gives us through our children is the chance to see things fresh and new. He uses them to shake us out of our old worn-out ideas and limitations.

For you, this may be the case with reading. Helping your child learn to read may awaken something in you that wasn't there before. If so, then as you teach your child, you too may discover a lifelong love of reading.

CHAPTER

1

Little Ones, Language, and Love:
Birth to Two Years

IN THE COZY CLOSENESS OF THE womb, a child is introduced to language through his mother's voice, and in the best of circumstances, his father's. The effect of this early exposure is obvious from the get-go. Newborns are more sensitive to human sounds than any others.

In addition to responding more readily to human voices, they show a marked preference for the sounds with which they've grown familiar prenatally. Amazingly, infants are born with an ear for their native tongue. Studies of four-day-old French babies found they responded more eagerly to French speakers than to Russian; for Russian babies, the opposite held true.

In the early days, mother's voice and father's, then brothers' and sisters', grandmas', grandpas'—all will surround the baby with love. And language.

From the beginning, language is based in intimacy. Mothers and fathers coo and sing to their babies while holding them close and snuggling. They even speak a different language from that which they speak with work associates or friends—what some experts have called *parentese*.

Have you ever noticed that? How adults pitch their voices higher when talk-ing to babies? People of every culture speaking every language use this method of "baby talk." We don't need to be told to do this; it happens almost instinctually. And there's a good reason for it: studies prove that babies turn their attention more readily to higher-pitched voices. In some unidentified way it's part of their preparation for human language.

LANGUAGE DEVELOPMENT BEGINS IN THE WOMB

Newborn infants show marked preferences.
- Babies are more responsive to human voices.
- Babies are more responsive to their native tongue.
- Babies are more responsive to their mother's (and often father's) voice.
- Babies are more responsive to higher-pitched voices.

The origins of human language are still a mystery to many secular linguists. Far and away more complex than that of other living creatures, human com-munication fascinates them. These linguists wonder—but will never completely understand—why the child understands the concept of *dada*, then speaks it. They speculate on how children are able to pick up the rules of their native tongue with no formal instruction. Some theorize a "learning program" in the brain's structure to explain how humans arrived at such sophistication. Humans, they think, must have a genetically determined predisposition for language and language structure that is part of the evolutionary process.

Yet something as intricate as language couldn't evolve spontaneously any more than Beethoven's symphonies or Duke Ellington's compositions could. There had to be a Grand Plan. *God gave us the gift of language.*

Lord knows we need it. Animals have instincts that compel them toward the behavior appropriate to their species: how to hide from enemies, build nests, protect, feed, and care for their young, finally to teach them to run or to fly.

Compare human infants with animal babies. Humans take almost a year to walk independently; horses walk and run within minutes of birth. In the animal kingdom, the young are helpless for only the briefest period, and their own development is governed by instinct. All their instinctual behaviors would be released even if they were kept in a solitary condition.

Not so with humans. We don't have many instincts. We have potentials—given to us by God—that can only be released if certain requirements are met within our environment. Unlike animals, human infants are completely dependent on their parents for many years. Most of their training is accomplished through language. The few documented cases of children who grew up apart from other humans, as well as studies of children raised in isolated or solitary conditions, describe individuals with limited human characteristics.

God must have had something in mind when he created us this way.

Comfort, Communication, and the Creator

Consider how significant a role language plays in God's plan for us. Language is so essential, so intricately woven into our humanness—could we really be human without it? Not if you consider how clearly God made us not to be alone.

Through his gift of language, God provided a basis for his best gift of all—relationship. He designed us to be deeply involved in each other's lives, and language is the medium of interdependence. The warm communication between parent and baby sets the stage for the development of language. In the absence of serious deficiencies, the beginning of language takes place in the context of love.

This loving context is critical to the child's later ability to communicate and trust. The assurance of mother love is essential to the optimum development of language in the child.

It begins with the baby's first cry. Even in his first wail, a baby expresses his individuality. Neonatal nurses know firsthand that even in hospital nurseries, each newborn has a distinctly personal cry. Mothers of many will attest that their babies varied in style, tone, and volume, each producing a unique cry.

Crying is really the baby's first form of communication. Where does crying come from? The newborn's cry is really a reflex reaction to discomfort. The baby is hungry or hurting. The world is alerted. His parents respond.

Baby's Speech and Language Development

Throughout the ages in diverse cultures, parents have responded unconditionally to babies' cries. In our own "sophisticated" culture, some wonder if that's the right thing to do, worrying that they'll spoil the baby. Still, most parents find their impulse is to respond, and this is another place—as it was with "parentese"—where your natural inclinations are right. It is important to respond to a baby's cries. It's part of God's plan for your relationship with your child, as your response sets the stage for a trusting relationship and good communication between you and your child.

In the early months of a baby's life, this unconditional response is crucial. When a baby cries from hunger or hurt and no one responds, he will not learn that communication is effective. He may give up, become listless (the sign of a baby in despair), like the babies we see from countries where the food supply never filters down to the most helpless.

Through having his needs met—hunger filled or comfort restored—the baby experiences communication as something that brings closeness and contentment. This positive beginning is damaged when parents ignore their infant's cries for the sake of "discipline." Discipline will come later and, hopefully, by more positive means. During the early months, parents need to pray for patience and for God to change their hearts to be able to accept their newborn's needs and "language" without reservation. They will reap the rewards later.

Body language is another big part of an infant's communication package. As he grows stronger, the baby uses every part of his body to speak. He waves his arms and hands, wiggles his torso, thrusts his face forward, turns toward or away from others. As he grows older, he signals wanting to be picked up, to be put down, needing more space—wordlessly, but unmistakably.

Meanwhile, the baby's cries become more differentiated and our ears become more attuned so that we begin to know if a cry means baby needs a feeding, a diaper change, comfort, or a nap. As we learn the baby's "language" and respond appropriately, he develops trust and confidence. Even in the earliest years, good communication builds stronger relationships.

ATTACHMENT PARENTING SETS THE STAGE FOR LOVING COMMUNICATION

Parenting programs aimed at imposing early discipline through scheduled infant feedings and limited cuddling time interfere with the infant's proper development—particularly in the area of language. A crying infant needs to be fed, changed, or perhaps just held. Reassuring him gives positive reinforcement to the only form of communication he has.

Dr. William Sears and his wife, Martha, practicing pediatrician and pediatric nurse, authors of twenty-two books on child rearing, and—perhaps most importantly—Christian parents of eight children, advocate "attachment parenting," creating a strong and loving bond between parent and infant. I recommend their comprehensive *Complete Book of Christian Parenting and Childcare* to get parents and babies off to the right start.

The other side of parent/child communication consists of the parents' vocalizations as they feed, bathe, and dress the baby. Though these may seem one-sided—the parent talking *to* the infant—they are vital, laying an early foundation for language development.

Any witness to that intense look of concentration from an infant concentrating faithfully on the words his mom or dad is speaking knows something important is going on. The baby is learning to listen—the other side of communication and language skills.

Baby's first smile is really his first attempt to communicate back something positive. No intellectual analysis will convey any more than the tremendous satisfaction a parent feels when he receives this coveted communication.

Cooing

Soon the infant begins to seem aware—in between the uncomfortable and unhappy times—that there is another state of being: contentment. He begins to express his contentment. He coos. His communication potential expands as his language is no longer limited to moments of discomfort, but to expressing pleasure also.

He feels contented, he makes noises of contentment. By at least occasionally responding to their baby's coos of contentment as well as to cries of discontent, parents help establish this positive side of communication in the child's early language. Again, communication builds relationship.

Clearly God designed language as something that would shape, express, and enhance our relationships. And, miraculously, no matter how difficult his native tongue, only two conditions are necessary for a child anywhere in the world to learn language:

1. intimacy with others, and
2. language in the environment.

Most of the time these happen without our even thinking about it. We take so much for granted. It's only when we see some part of the process disrupted, as for instance with a handicapped, institutionalized, or economically disadvantaged child, that we begin to appreciate that though millions of children all over the world are cooing for the first time today, their numbers don't make it any less a miracle.

From that first coo, each child will arrive at adulthood with a vocabulary of twenty thousand to fifty thousand words and appropriate syntax (which we'll discuss later) for his particular language.

But that's a long look ahead. There's so much more to do before he gets there.

Babababa–Babbling

At four to five months, the child enters the stage of language acquisition known as *babbling* (I have found enormous satisfaction while researching for this book that even the experts use the same terms we do for the first two stages: cooing and babbling). Now the child begins to experiment with his lips and tongue to change the sounds he makes: babababa, mumumumu, gagagaga, dododododo.

The amazing aspect about this stage is that in random babbling the baby proves capable of producing *every* sound of *every* language.

So if at five months we are capable of reproducing every sound, why is it so hard in high school to pronounce the *u* in the French word *tu* (which my French teacher urged us to say properly by rounding our lips and saying *ee*—what a concept!)? Or how about rolling *rrrr*'s in Spanish, *ch* as in the German *ich*, not to mention the intonations and (to us) unusual sounds of Chinese, Japanese, and a host of Asian languages?

The unmistakable fact is that in acquiring our own language, we lose a lot. As the child plays and practices a huge repertoire of sounds, he begins to let go of some. He concentrates and holds on to only those sounds he hears in his environment, discarding those that are not part of his native language.

This is why with no special effort a child in a bilingual home can learn two languages and speak them fluently. For children, all languages are equally easy to learn. As adults, on the other hand, we find some languages easier to learn than others. It's not just the vocabulary and sentence structure that challenge us, but also these discarded *phonemes* (linguistic lingo for the sounds that are the building blocks of language). No matter how well we master, say Japanese, it's safe to say no one will take us for a native.

Still, though the words and even the basic sounds of each language are different, there are universal patterns followed by every child in acquiring his native tongue. No matter the culture or language, every able child follows the same developmental sequence.

LANGUAGE MILESTONES

2 to 4 weeks:	cooing
4 to 6 weeks:	smiling (nonverbal communication)
6 to 12 months:	babbling (undifferentiated sounds), followed by deliberate mimicking
1 year or so:	single words
2 years or so:	two-word utterances leading to simple sentences

---

During the babbling stage, children love making sounds, putting consonants and vowels together for the sheer joy of it. Once a child begins deliberate mimicking, his language will become specific.

At this stage, the parent can help stimulate growth toward communication by repeating sounds back to the child. Again, this is a pattern most people fall into without any conscious effort: Baby says "babababababa," and daddy or mommy repeats it, pausing to see if the baby will say some more. He usually does. This give and take—pausing between vocalizations then reflecting back what baby has said—is the child's first experience with conversational language.

During the mimicking stage, the child begins to also recognize the metrical patterns of his native tongue. In France, where the accent is usually on the last syllable, six-month-old babies show a preference for such words. Their American counterparts, however, are more responsive to words with stressed first syllables, such as *mommy* and *daddy* and *baby* and *doggy*.

While the child is still doing a lot of exploring with sounds during the mimicking stage, he is also beginning to modulate and practice more control.

TYPICAL ORDER OF ORAL SOUNDS

b, d, p, m, n, t, and vowels
g, k, ng, w, h, j
f, v, th, sh, ch, s, z, r, l
Blends: tr, pl, br, st, sw

Baby's First Word

One of the highlights of baby's first year is his first word. Not a random *mama* or *dada* ("Did he really know he was calling me, honey?"), but a word unmistakably connected to the specific person or object. Keep in mind that a child's first word may not be a true word. But if your pet terrier steps into the room and your baby squeals in delight and says, "Goggy!" then that is as good a word as they come.

Now the parent can reflect back what the child has said with a slight variation, "Yes, doggy." Keep it short and simple, only two words—an acknowledgment and the correct pronunciation. Use encouragement—a conversational rather than corrective tone of voice. Your acceptance of his first words encourages the child and makes him eager to try more. This principle of reflecting back without specifically correcting is the way to handle all language development through the early years.

Keep in mind that no matter how important, language is only one part of your child's total development, and there is much going on in the first year. There are advances in gross motor control, fine motor control, sensory perception—many different areas. Try to stay relaxed and happy with your child, not pushing unless for some reason (as in the case of babies with Down syndrome) your child needs it.

Try not to compare your child, unless you see specific red flags—significantly large delays in meeting developmental milestones (see appendix C). In these cases, you want to obtain intervention services as quickly as possible. But remember that you will always see a broad range of language development among children. Having opportunities to be around a lot of children the same age as your own—in play groups, volunteering in the church nursery—can help keep things in perspective.

By the end of the first year, most babies are saying a word or two in addition to calling Mommy and Daddy by name. But that's only one side of their language ability.

Every child really has two vocabularies: active and passive. The *active vocabulary* (sometimes called expressive language) consists of words the child is able to say, as when he points to a tank in the pet store and says "fish." The *passive vocabulary* (sometimes called receptive language) consists of words the child understands when others speak them, as when Grandpa says, "Where is Timmy's nose?" and little Timmy points to his nose without speaking. When we say that a one-year-old's vocabulary is made up of two words, then, we're talking only of words he actually says, not of words he actually knows. Throughout the preschool years the child's passive vocabulary is much greater than his active one.

It may not occur naturally to parents to provide their children with a lot of words at this period of their development; after all, what they see is a child working on *mommy, daddy, bye-bye, doggie, cat,* and *fish.* But the creation of a language-rich environment is important even in the early years.

CREATING A LANGUAGE-RICH ENVIRONMENT FOR INFANTS

If you could raise your child's IQ through doses of some special elixir, you'd do it in a heartbeat—no matter how awful the taste.

How wonderful then that getting our children off to a good start is such a sweet thing to accomplish. Try these good old-fashioned methods:

Lullabies

Nursery rhymes—Jack and Jill, Humpty Dumpty, etc.

Repetitive songs—Old McDonald, the Wheels on the Bus, etc.

Finger plays

Naming—everything at home, at the zoo, at the beach, out the car
 window

Picture books

Puppets and stuffed animals "talking" to the child

If you're a talker naturally, keeping up a conversation with your baby will come naturally. If you grew up in a home with younger children and were able to observe good parenting there, baby conversation will be a breeze. But if you're on the quiet side and haven't had a role model, you may need to make a conscious effort to learn to talk to your baby. Start by talking naturally, describing what you and your baby are doing:

"Shake, shake, shake the rattle!"

"Put it in the basket."

"Let's eat lunch."

"Up, up, up we go!"

"Where's the baby?"

"Up in the high chair."

"Put on your bib."

"Mommy's making cereal."

Use short sentences and a lot of inflection. While holding your gaze steady on baby, say a few words, ask a question, then pause to give the baby a chance to "talk" back to you. His response may be arm waving or grunting or cooing, but it's sure to show his excitement. This is the beginning of conversation—taking turns expressing feelings and listening.

Make it a practice to name everything in baby's sight: spoon, kitty, banana, cup. Long before he can speak, the child is storing up many words. The more he comes in contact with, the more he'll have at his disposal when the time comes for him to explode into language.

Shortly after his first birthday, the child develops the physical control of the mouth and tongue necessary to produce words at will. Because he is now walking and climbing, he is learning more and more about things in his environment. You will notice imitative behavior, such as jabbering on the phone.

At eighteen months or so, you will witness what is best described as a language explosion. After slow but steady progress, he suddenly begins acquiring words at the mind-boggling rate of ten to twelve per day. As always, understanding always outpaces vocalization: most will remain part of his passive vocabulary for a long time before they become part of his spoken language. Still, the richer the passive vocabulary, the better for the child.

Usually before the second birthday another amazing development takes place; you might be ready to leave the house but caught up in a last-minute search for keys when your little one grows impatient and demands, "Go now." A developmental milestone has been reached. It is baby's first sentence. Again you acknowledge,

"Yes, we are going now, but we need our keys." After all, maybe he knows where they are!

Reading Tips

Books are the best! Even if you never really connected with reading before, you may discover as a parent, through reading with your own little one, that it's a lot of fun. One of the greatest benefits of having kids is the opportunity it gives us to grow and to change. The first step to putting your child on the path to a lifelong love of reading is to fall in love with reading yourself.

Actually falling in love with reading isn't that hard to do. Take it from someone who's been reading to kids for thirty-six years: children's books are fun to read—especially when you know what to look for.

Looking for the *right* books is important. There's a lot out there to choose from. And there's a lot to avoid. If you're going to take the time to cuddle up and read a book to your child—especially if your time is limited—why not make it the best?

What makes some books better than others? Here's what C. S. Lewis, author of *The Lion, the Witch, and the Wardrobe* and five other books in the beloved Narnia series, has to say: "I never wrote down to anyone . . . it certainly is my opinion that a book worth reading only in childhood is not worth reading even then."[3]

To start with, the best children's literature, like all literature, presents some problem that needs resolution, as in *Caps for Sale*, in which the cap seller must get his caps back from the rascally monkeys. In the end the story shows how the problem is resolved and reestablishes feelings of security and well-being, as in *Good Dog, Carl*. Better yet, it will teach a lesson, very subtly, along the way, as in *Where's Our Mama?*, which reminds children to stay in the same place when they are lost, while validating each listener's belief that his mama is the best.

Don't Tell Me, Show Me

Many very entertaining and engaging stories carry an extra bonus: a theme that reinforces a value or virtue. The message in *The Rainbow Fish* may be clear to adults: pride isolates a person, and sharing feels good. Even though the theme is never stated directly, we can easily put it into words ourselves. The child's mind works differently. A statement of theme would mean nothing to them. But through the story of the rainbow fish's conflict and resolution, the theme can have a powerful impact on the character of a child.

Children, especially, think and perceive on a concrete level. During the preschool years they are incapable of abstract thinking. Teaching them about kindness, generosity, courage, etc., can only take place through stories.

Most of us—children and adults—would rather have someone *show* why something works than *tell* them. Very few of us enjoy being clobbered with ideas. We'd rather hear stories. Experts refer to the themes underlying plot lines as subliminal messages. For Christians, the Holy Spirit undoubtedly has a hand in shaping us through well-presented stories. That's why the parables of Jesus are so powerful.

Rhythm and Repetition

Two characteristics you will often find in children's books are rhythm and repetition. Both work to keep the child focused on the book. Skillful children's authors know this will keep a child coming back again and again. As you read, emphasize the rhythm and repetition in the text. Besides making a book more fun for you and your child, each also makes it easy for the child to memorize the text and "read" it on his own.

Even if your baby's still very young and not yet capable of understanding the words, you can still use these guidelines when you select books for him, especially books you are buying to build a library.

GUIDELINES FOR BUYING BOOKS

With an unlimited budget for books, you could build a library of everything out there for kids. Thank goodness our budgets are limited. That way we are forced to look for the best!

Is the book attractive to children?

Is this book fun to read—over and over again?

Does this book have staying power—a timeless theme or classic message?

Does this book reinforce (or at least not challenge) the values I want for my family?

Does this book invite parent-child interaction?

Is the author of this book speaking to children and not to their parents?

If you can afford it, I do heartily recommend building a home library (see appendix E for discount sources). When your children see you buying books, they realize that books have value and worth. There are many inexpensive paperback editions out—with the same wonderful illustrations as the expensive hardbacks—that for the cost of a video rental, you can get a book or two to have around for many years.

Books are a worthy investment. Children treat books like old friends: they want to spend a lot of time with the ones they really enjoy. No child's book is ever read just once. Children return again and again to a favorite book rather than losing interest or outgrowing it. They pore over the pictures, discovering new details, thinking to themselves and talking to each other about them.

Trust me, a good book will hold your child's attention much longer than most toys, and they have the advantage of not missing pieces or cluttering up your house as much. Books also have a longer lifespan than toys. Books have a way of growing up with a child. I've heard of college-bound teens who've asked their parents

Reading together builds relationships.

not to get rid of their own childhood libraries—they want them for their own children.

Check secondhand stores and garage sales for used books. But do make sure they are in good repair before buying them. If you bring books with torn or drawn on pages into your home, it will give your child the idea that these things are OK. If you want your child to respect books, they must be in good condition.

Let grandparents, friends, and family know that you would love to receive books for baby gifts. If you have several children and they receive books for gifts, you will build a respectable library faster than you think.

Public libraries are a good resource for borrowing books (they also have sales of old books sometimes), and trips to the library have a lot of charm. But here you would be wise to give your child a lot of guidance. There are many books out that have themes incompatible with the needs of children and perhaps with your own convictions. I always page through books my children pick before actually checking them out. I have weeded out some real junk that way.

If your library has a story hour, check to see which book the librarian is reading before taking your child. Stories about witches, goblins, and ghosts for instance (standard fare during Halloween season) are never appropriate for toddlers, who are not yet capable of distinguishing between reality and fantasy.

Those are issues you will face later on. Books for babies are straightforward and innocent—pictures of familiar things, or stories like *Goodnight Moon,* which just sound irresistible.

In the beginning, you may want to start with board books. These are the more indestructible editions, with heavy unbendable pages. Between readings, I keep ours in a basket on the floor. You might want to do this also so your own little one can choose them at playtime even when you're not right beside him.

Cuddle Up

From the time you can hold your baby in a sitting position, both of you can share the joy of reading together. Reading before bedtime is a wonderful tradition to begin early on, but try not to limit reading to only one time—try after lunch or after playtime. In addition to spending quality time, you will be planting some pre-reading skills that will help him later on. Early read-alouds build good listening habits, laying the foundation for a child who can cooperate and concentrate, who will develop good comprehension skills.

So do start early!

While holding your baby in your lap, look at the book in front of you together at a comfortable level. Exaggerate the care with which you pick up just the corner of the page and turn it. If the text seems too complicated, use your own words—but remember, the child's ability to understand is always well beyond the words he can say. Your voice and inflection play an important part in his understanding. As you read the text, point, sliding your finger smoothly just under the words.

What is going on? In addition to the warm closeness and the sharing of a story as well as possibly a message, you are also laying the groundwork for your child to respect books and treat them carefully. Through the left-to-right

Daddy's voice is very special.

movement of the text, you are planting some subtle information: reading is left to right across the page, one line follows another, and we read the left page before the right.

That so much valuable learning could be going on during such a pleasant interlude is like icing on the cake—and all the more reason to find those moments to read with your child.

Book Recommendations

If you are new parents and just beginning your adventure into the world of children's books, hold on to your hats!

There are years of fun ahead for you and your children!

After thirty-six years of reading books to my own children as well as to students, I know which books deserve more than a casual read or two, which can

When the words are too complicated, use your own.

please now and later, and which can even stand up to a few hundred readings (don't laugh until you've had a few children!).

With twelve children and two parents who love books, our family has built quite a children's library—close to two thousand volumes. They line a wall and a half in my office. Along with a cozy couch, they invite my children to read while Mama writes.

All this by way of saying, I didn't have to go very far to find these book recommendations. To share the best and brightest in children's books with you, I've simply pulled out the best from my own children's shelves.

The fact that some were pretty worn—having spent a lot of time in children's laps and hands—made them easier to sight on the shelves. I left behind their wallflower cousins and chose the ones whose dance cards were always full.

In my recommendations, I have listed the date of first publication so you get a sense of the timelessness of stories with true kid appeal. However, I checked carefully to make sure that each book I've recommended is currently in print and available. You will find them on the shelves or by order through your local library or bookstore, or on the Internet through www.amazon.com (where used copies are sometimes available for under a dollar) and/or www.christianbook.com.

These books have been a major part of my life for thirty-five years. So it is with great pleasure that I introduce these faithful family friends. As you get to know them, I am sure you will love them too.

Six Months to Two Years

BOARD BOOKS

There are shopping carts full of board books available, but they seem to appear and disappear a little more quickly than other children's books. For this reason, I am recommending my very favorites that promise to be around for a while.

Also, each year, more and more children's classics such as *Goodnight, Moon; Runaway Bunny;* or *Corduroy* are being released in board book format. Browse through the children's section of your bookstore to see what's available. Buying a classic in board book form (as long as it isn't condensed) means your investment will add up to more years of reading.

Since I'll be reviewing classics later in the age-appropriate lists, the following are just a few family favorites published only in board editions:

All Aboard Noah's Ark (also *In the Beginning, Baby Moses, Jonah and the Whale, Little David and the Giant* and all the Chunky Board Book series) by Mary Josephs, Golden Inspirational, 1994.

Small, pudgy books fit well in small, pudgy hands, with little flaps to peek under on every page. Each tells a familiar story in simple, childish language.

Make board books available at baby's level.

The Baby Bible Story Book, Robin Currie, Cook Communications, 1994.

Bible stories scaled for the smallest, with lots of interactive opportunities (pretending to hammer while Noah builds the ark, clapping hands as Noah closes the door behind the animals, wiggling fingers for the rain). Each draws a simple conclusion and offers a child's prayer. Cute illustrations.

Little Duck's Friends (also others in the series of Squeeze-and-Squeak Books) by Muff Singer, Joshua Morris, 1994.

Special pages cut around a soft plastic duck invite the child to press and make him squeak. The story line explains, in rhyme, how each animal has special gifts. So does baby!

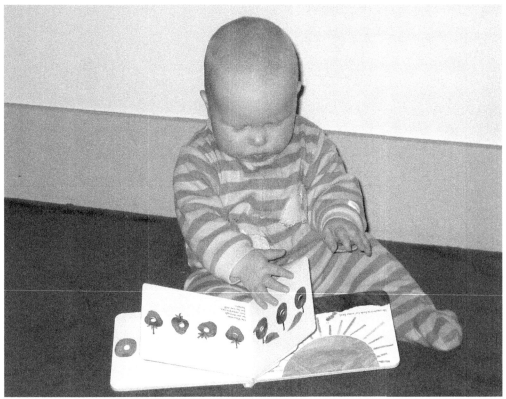

Board books encourage concentration and independence.

Pat the Bunny by Dorothy Kunhardt, Golden Press, 1940.

With more than seven million copies sold since its first publication, this book remains in its original condition and is a favorite shower gift. An unabashedly old-fashioned and delightful book with lots of "fingers on" fun for tots.

Toes, Ears, and Nose, and *Where's Baby's Belly Button?* Karen Katz, Little Simon, 2003.

By an author who knows how to reach children, these books are great for warm fuzzy interaction with a little one.

Read-Aloud Stories

While these books can captivate the attention of very young children, their appeal and value extend well beyond these early years. A four- or five-year-old will find much of interest in Richard Scarry's *Best Word Book Ever,* for example. Other books, such as *Caps for Sale* or *Noisy Nora,* will later double as your child's first readers.

Best Word Book Ever, Richard Scarry, Golden Books, 1963.

Every one of my children—from the oldest (now thirty-six) to the current toddlers—has found plenty to hold the attention for hours in this terrific vocabulary builder, chock-full of pictures of almost everything a child could possibly learn to name.

Brown Bear, Brown Bear, What Do You See? Bill Martin Jr., illustrated by Eric Carle, Holt and Company, 1967.

A story built on rhythm and repetition, highlighting colors and animals, little ones love this first memory stretcher.

Caps for Sale, Esphyr Slobodkina, Scholastic, 1940.

Be dramatic! Shake your fists! Stomp your feet! You and your toddler will have much fun with this wonderful story in which common sense prevails over temper tantrums!

Chicken Soup with Rice, Maurice Sendak, Scholastic, 1962.

Another R&R (rhythm and repetition)—this one filled with a feeling of humor. Impossible to read without a smile.

Good Dog, Carl, Alexandra Day, Simon & Schuster, 1985.

A wonderful introduction to story sequence—plot, scenes, characters, emotion (Will they get the house in order before Mother comes home?)—all without a single word of text! Toddlers and parents can have a lot of fun with this engagingly illustrated tale.

Goodnight Moon, Margaret Wise Brown, Harper & Row, 1947.

If you could do a survey of children's favorite books and ask children themselves, this gem of a book would surely top the list. A bunny gets ready for sleep, saying goodnight to each special object he sees from his bed. A soft and soothing farewell at the end of any little one's busy day.

Jamberry, Bruce Degen, Harperfestival, 1985.

An energetic romp through the colorful world of berries with a rollicking rhyme-spouting bear and a straw-hatted boy. There's so much to celebrate!

"More More More" Said the Baby, Vera B. Williams, William Morrow & Co., 1990.

A trio of love stories—three toddlers enjoying tender moments with father, grandmother, and mother. Catchy toddler words, bright vivid pictures. Natural, wholesome, current, very appealing.

Noisy Nora, Rosemary Wells, Scholastic, 1973.

Poor Nora! The loveable mousette experiences all the pangs of the child-in-the-middle, caught between the demands of baby brother and bossiness of big sister. Catchy meter, playful illustrations make for a wonderfully satisfying mouse's tale.

On Mother's Lap, Ann Herbert Scott, Scholastic, 1992.

An Eskimo boy finds a lot of room on mother's lap for all his favorite things, but thinks there's none for baby sister. Mother shows him there's room for all. A wonderful remedy for new-baby blues.

Read-Aloud Bible Stories, volumes 1–4, Ella K. Lindvall, Moody, 1982–95

These large volumes with bold full-page illustrations on one side, simple text on the other have a lot of kid appeal. One unusual feature is that Jesus' face is never seen, thus avoiding some of the stereotypes and allowing room for children's imagination. Bible stories retold with rhythm, repetition, and loads of enthusiasm: e.g., when the apostles fish where Jesus tells them: *"Big fish / little fish / wiggly fish / Oh my!"*

The Runaway Bunny, Margaret Wise Brown, Harper & Row, 1942.

Another must-have from the author of *Goodnight Moon*, the story of every-bunny, who—like every typical toddler—wants to assert his independence from mother while being reminded she will always be there for him. Beautifully illus-trated, a message with lasting value.

Shoes, Elizabeth Winthrop, Harper & Row, 1986.

A rollicking rhyming tribute to a toddler's most-loved item of apparel. Just for fun!

The Toddler's Bible, V. Gilbert Beers, Cook Communications, 2004.

Straight through the Bible, toddler-style. The author's ability to translate com-plex stories into a few simple sentences is sure to delight. Read this during the tod-dler years, and before you know it, your toddler will be reading it back to you.

The Very Hungry Caterpillar (also *The Very Busy Spider*, *The Grouchy Ladybug*, etc.), Eric Carle, Philomel Books, 1984.

A children's library with no books by Eric Carle would be like a chocolate chip cookie with no chips. This author understands how to captivate even the most easily distracted child. Read this one with lots of finger drama and chomping noises and your child is sure to be delighted.

Where's Our Mama? Diane Goode, Scholastic, 1991.

Such a sweet story! Two children who have lost their mama have trouble finding her only because they see her as the best, the wisest, the most beautiful. The gendarme (French policeman) is astonished to find that finally she is just a mama like everyone else's. For fun, read it with your best French accent!

°°° Check 🍎 for expanded list.°°°

CHAPTER

2

Learning to Read the Natural Way:
Two to Five Years

Now We're Talkin'

AT TWO THE REAL LANGUAGE EXPLOSION begins, making the preceding months look more like warning tremors than the real thing. The child now has a wide range of two-word sentences—and two words can say so much!

> Two-word sentences can:
>
> - Identify ("See duck!")
> - Claim ("My mommy.")
> - Ask ("Where Daddy?")
> - Describe ("Good yogurt.")

At two years of age, a child has approximately a 270-word vocabulary. This will quadruple in the next year.

Expressive Vocabulary

12 months—3 words

15 months—19 words

18 months—22 words

21 months—120 words

24 months—270 words

3 years—1000 words

Adult—20,000 to 60,000 words

Don't forget, a child understands at least twice as many words as he speaks!

Keep in mind that these ages are approximate, that even twins raised together will exhibit differences in timetables. Language development takes place while the child is learning many other skills:

- gross motor

- fine motor

- self-reliance

- social

Factors in Language Development

Sex (girls develop at a faster rate than boys)

Birth order

Intelligence

Overall health

Structure of mouth

Home environment

Of all the influences in language development, the only one over which parents have control is the atmosphere in the home. How a child's parents relate to him is all-important. In fact, it is more important than their education level. Regardless of background, any parent who wants to give his or her child the best can commit to creating an environment rich in language opportunities.

You can encourage your child's speech best through approval and carrying the conversational ball. Talk about everything. Look for the details around you: point to the flowers, the clouds, the sights from the car. If you grew up in a conversational home and are conversational yourself, this may come naturally to you. But for those who need some ideas for putting a little more *oomph* in communicating with little ones, here are some suggestions:

While working to enrich your child's conversation, continue expanding his vocabulary, providing words for everything in sight. As often as possible, take your child with you shopping. Go to the zoo, the country, the city. Look through magazines and catalogs together. Give him as many names as you can.

GIVE CLEAR COMMANDS

Efforts to expand sentences are best when they sharpen focus rather than add confusion. Keep commands short and direct.

Not: *"I want you to take care of putting these toys where they belong."*

But: *"Please pick up these toys."*

Can you hear the difference? Then your child will also.

Remember, a child's expressive language is only a portion of the words he has stored in his memory—and during the toddler years his mind is like a sponge, soaking up everything it touches. Just as God gave Adam mastery over the animals by giving him the responsibility of naming them, your child's ability to name things makes him feel confident of his place in the world.

TODDLER TALK TIPS

Rule Number One: Never correct a child's speech directly.

Rule Number Two: Use normal conversation to model correct form.

Add adjectives

    Child: *My ball.*

    Parent: *Yes, that is your big, blue ball.*

Fill in the blanks

    Child: *Cat out.*

    Parent: *Yes, the cat is going outside.*

Refine verb tense

    Child: *Duck swim.*

    Parent: *Yes, the duck is swimming.*

Expand thought

    Child: *Milk gone.*

    Parent: *Yes, you drank all the milk and it is gone!*

Stretch sentences into paragraphs

    Child: *Daddy bye-bye.*

    Parent: *Yes, Daddy went to work in his car. He'll be back at dinnertime.*

Ask questions

    Parent: *What will you do when Daddy comes home?*

WORDS, WORDS, WORDS

Your child's curiosity level will never be higher than during the toddler years. Language opportunities are all around:

Colors	Vehicles
Numbers	Rhyming words
Community helpers	Movement words (jump, hop)
Feelings	Relational words (in, under)
Parts of the body	Opposites (off/on)

Still, God created language for more important reasons than stewardship. He also gave us language to enable us to build strong relationships—with each other and with him. From the earliest years, a child needs to learn to be comfortable with the language of feelings: to use words to express emotions, seek comfort, and to cope with problems.

"Are you upset because Tommy doesn't want to share his truck? Maybe we should give him more time."

"Are you worried about the new Sunday school class? Everybody worries the first time. I'll make sure the teachers know who you are before I leave."

"Are you afraid when the lights are off at night? Did you know Daddy and I are here and you're safe while you're asleep?"

LITTLE ONES LOGIC 101

Begin early to build your child's reasoning skills. Show how through language you cope with the unexpected: "Since it's raining, we can't go out today like we planned. That's disappointing, isn't it? What could we do instead? Maybe we could invite Grandma over."

In this simple way, a mom has

- acknowledged a problem
- acknowledged her child's feelings
- shown that we can take charge of the situation so as to not feel like a victim
- offered an attractive alternative

During this time of intense language acquisition, parents do well to drop all baby talk and consistently model correct speech. Using complete sentences calls the child up to the next level:

Instead of "Daddy go bye-bye."

Try "Daddy's going bye-bye."

Or better: "Daddy's going to work."

As a toddler, my oldest son, Joshua, had some interesting pronunciations of words. He said *panacake* instead of pancake, *hamgurber* instead of hamburger, and *theetyer* instead of theater. His big sisters, as well as his parents, found this so amusing we never corrected him. In fact, we enjoyed his new words so much we started using them at home ourselves. Only when he got into an argument with younger brother Matthew about the correct pronunciation (Joshua was insisting we were eating *panacakes*) did we realize we had carried on the joke a little too long.

Use clear pronunciation and a pleasant tone of voice. Remember, you are modeling how you want your child to talk to others. After years of being TV-free (see appendix D) even when we did sign up for satellite service to take advantage of all the educational shows, I did not allow my children to watch sitcoms on major networks because the characters' tone of voice is usually sarcastic, argumentative, whiny, or disrespectful. Children sound like what they're used to listening to. As I pointed out in *Mommy, Teach Me!* children are "little mirrors." Down to the smallest details, they are reflections of us. If you say *sumthin'* instead of *something*, your children probably will also.

GIVE YOUR CHILD A HEAD START IN SPEECH

You are the first speech teacher your child has—you could be the best!

- Pronounce clearly but comfortably.
- Keep the volume down.
- Speak at a comfortable pace—not too fast or too slow.
- Use a pleasant tone of voice.
- Choose interesting vocabulary—but not more than one step above your child's level.

Of our twelve children, three are married, two are in college, and one is living independently. That leaves six still at home. Add in ten grandchildren and whichever of the kids' friends shows up and you can imagine what the crowd is like for Sunday family dinners. You can also imagine, since most of the twenty-seven are far from quiet and reserved, the decibel level—like a party where the noise level keeps rising as each person tries to talk over the background conversations. When our dinner table starts getting a little too loud for my taste, I just start whispering. Since I would like my children to be a little more soft-spoken I try (keyword *try*) to keep my own voice down.

Always remember to use the most subtle and indirect form to correct your child's immature speech—modeling the right way yourself, very casually, conversationally:

> **Child:** "See fishy over dere."
> **Parent:** "Yes, I see the fish over there."
> **Child:** "Pitty cat."
> **Parent:** "Yes, that is a pretty cat."

Don't try to force your child to say things correctly. Sometimes he can't. Some consonant sounds and combinations are actually very sophisticated and appear rather late developmentally.

And so much is going on! Even as your child is acquiring vocabulary at an astonishing rate, even as he continues to perfect his pronunciation, he is also absorbing the syntax of our language. Syntax is the way our language is organized to convey information; these are the rules that enable us to communicate with understanding.

Here is another dimension of human speech that leaves the "experts" with as many questions as answers. Since each language has a different syntax (rules governing sentence arrangement, plurals, word tenses, etc.), linguists can say only that we are born with the capacity to absorb the syntax of our native tongue. But they don't know how it happens.

Again, I see God's hand clearly.

And you will too as you watch your child absorbing the surprises and subtleties of the English language. You won't need to sit down and give your child formal lessons in grammar. Simply by listening, he will pick up the rules.

As he learns the rules, he will adhere to them rigidly. What will you think when he runs in to tell you: "Mommy, the cat bringed in two mouses!"

Maybe you'll recognize that this represents a great deal of sophistication for your child. He has learned

- that verbs have tenses (adding -*ed* means it already happened), and

- that nouns have plurals (adding *s* shows there is more than one of something).

No small accomplishment! And all without a single direct lesson from you.

Now, your job is not to correct him, but to gently lead him further into the subtleties I mentioned simply by modeling. Ideally, your child should never even notice what you have done when you reflect back: "Oh, honey, let's go see. The cat brought in two mice?"

Practicing this type of correction will keep your child comfortable as he's learning to communicate. Remember, he *wants* to do well. Children have feelings as real as ours. They also feel embarrassed when they make mistakes, less sure of themselves later. Give your child the best start by keeping communication encouraging and positive.

LISTENING SKILLS

Don't forget to help your child develop good listening skills too!
Early on, teach him to look directly at the person who is speaking.
Whisper in his ear and ask him to repeat what you have said.
Ask questions about stories you have read.
And most important of all: Listen to him!

Keep in mind that one child's language development may appear to take place as a smooth progression from words to short phrases to sentences. Another child may travel a different learning curve: spurts of rapid development followed by plateaus, or even some regression. Remember, boys are generally six months or so behind girls in language development during the preschool years.

In addition, a child may experience upheavals that will set back or slow down his development for a while—the birth of a sibling, a family move, a grandparent's death. Try to accept your child's individual development pattern. Don't compare him to other children. And try not to pressure him in the area of language.

If your preschool child at any time begins to stutter, do both yourself and him a favor: don't take it too seriously. A child's mind goes through periods where it races along faster than his organs of speech. One of my sons, now eighteen, went through four or five bouts of stuttering before he was nine. I think it's because he is a near-genius and his brain has always been in higher gear than his mouth. When the stutter appeared, we just became more patient—and we instructed his brothers and sisters to do the same. We let him take as long as he needed to say what he wanted to say. He didn't need our help.

Zach was also a late talker and a rather late reader among my kids (six or seven), yet he graduated two years early as a National Merit Scholarship finalist. He is a real example of the different individual timetables I mentioned earlier. Back in the days when he was struggling so hard to get out a single word, who would have guessed the gifts God had hidden inside? All I know is that when he was around ten or so, I remembered his stuttering and wondered where it had gone and when was the last time around.

Stuttering can disappear suddenly or gradually, but more often than not it does disappear—provided parents have not made an issue of it (see appendix F).

FRUSTRATION FACTORS

Anyone who ever suffered at the hands of an overly demanding foreign language teacher (like my own first French teacher, God rest her hard-to-please soul) can sympathize with how kids feel when they experience any of the following:

- high expectations
- pushing
- overcorrecting
- teasing, poking fun

Avoid these little spoilers. *Use the Golden Rule with your children* and you will never go wrong.

Most importantly, enjoy! Accept and appreciate where your child is in his language development. Don't push; just invite him along on the journey to better speech through modeling and expanding. *Keep his early language based on love and good feelings*, just as it was in infancy.

Remember, reading is simply putting together symbols to produce the words you've usually already heard. Give your child the warmest and richest early language experience you can and he will bring those positive feelings with him to the written word as well.

Reading: Time to Begin

When is the best time to start thinking about how your child will learn to read?

Now!

Who is the best teacher?

You.

You've already gotten some idea how important and qualified a teacher you are. After all, God entrusted you to pass on his gift of language to your child. If your heart's desire is to continue the natural progression of spoken language into writing and reading, he will give you the confidence you need to do it.

Never forget, you are your child's number one role model. He wants so much to be like you. If he sees you reading, if you have had cozy times reading together, he will naturally want to learn to read himself. Why wait to let someone else fulfill that wish?

It's a wonderful feeling to listen to a child read whom you have taught yourself, especially when that child is your own. And awesome to know he will be able to enjoy reading for years to come—eventually to your grandchildren.

I know this feeling from experience. And I also know teaching your child to read is not as difficult as most people think.

The next half of this chapter will give you all you need to teach your children the skills they need to begin a lifelong love of reading. I can't stress enough, you are already your child's primary teacher. Teaching reading is like the icing on the cake.

In the following pages, you will

- discover keys to unlock your child's reading potential.

- be liberated from the "teaching mystique" which convinces us that people need a credential to teach children a basic skill they themselves have used daily for decades.

- learn a few simple exercises, that at the very least, will develop your child's pre-reading skills to give him a head start in school.

- be inspired to carry it all the way through.

Be confident of this: With a little consistency and faithful effort, you can teach your child to read before he goes to school—or at least give him the head start that will make the critical difference between success and failure.

Why start early?

In our country, we are accustomed to thinking of children learning to read in first grade, or perhaps kindergarten. If you have always assumed that six is the appropriate age to begin reading, you may wonder why it would be wise to begin earlier.

Remember our discussion of sensitive periods? These are certain ages when the window of opportunity is widest for releasing the child's potential abilities.

Book displays encourage reading.

The sensitive period for learning reading skills is usually between the ages of four and five.

The word *usually* is important, because for all children, in every phase of their development, there is a wide range of variation. Having been a mother of toddlers for three decades, as well as a preschool teacher, I know that very well. You can't push a child to do something he is not developmentally ready to do.

However, the more you understand how to meet the needs of the sensitive period and the wider you try to open that window, the more likely you are to see a smooth transition as the potential is released.

What this means for you, practically speaking, is that if you have three children and you put the simple *Mommy, Teach Me to Read!* ideas into practice, you may wind up with three different outcomes as each child reaches school age:

- one five-year-old who reads fluently;

- one who is reading-ready, with full command of phonetic sounds, ready to combine them into words; and

- one who, even after a lot of practice, is still just beginning to know his sounds.

Does this mean that even though you put the same amount of effort into each of your children, you have succeeded with only one? Not at all! It just means that they were all on different timetables.

Does this mean that your time has been wasted on those you decide to send to school who will finish learning to read there? Absolutely not!

In fact, your efforts may have been best spent on the one child who has come nowhere near to reading. Let me explain.

The child who learned to read easily would probably have learned to read easily at school. The child who enters school on the brink of reading will probably finish learning to read with little effort. But the third child, the one who has learned only a few phonetic sounds—and perhaps with a great deal of effort on your part—will enter school in much better shape than he would have with no previous exposure to letters and sounds.

We teach reading early because most children can learn easily and enjoy reading right away, but also because it is best for the few children who might otherwise later be labeled as having learning difficulties.

Reading specialist Toni S. Gould explains it best:

> For the past thirty-five years I have tutored four- and five-year-old children who have been diagnosed as having learning disabilities. Those children needed a great deal more help with learning sound-letter correspondence than allowed for in kindergarten or first grade. At the preschool level they had the free time to learn and to develop an interest in learning. Without exception, they experienced success in learning to read.
>
> In contrast, children with identical learning problems who were referred to me after they experienced failure had a harder time learning because of the initial blow to their self-esteem. Tragically, they need not have failed and would not have failed if [they had been] taught reading-readiness skills, especially sound-letter knowledge.[4]

The Sound Game and the Letter Game, which I will share later in this chapter, will give each of your children a foundation of early success. If you enjoy them and do them on a regular basis, you will probably have a reader on your hands—and there is no thrill like hearing a child read whom you taught yourself.

But even if you do them on a less consistent basis, or even if your child is—like my own daughter Sophia—on a different developmental timetable, your time will be well spent. Even a child who can recognize ten phonetic sounds and six letters will enter school with a head start.

What becomes of early readers?

"What of the child who knows how to read before kindergarten? Won't he be bored when he enters school?" is a question that comes up sometimes for parents of preschoolers. After all, if it would be detrimental to the child's later academic success, you wouldn't want to spend the time teaching him too early.

It is safe to say that early reading is never harmful. For homeschoolers, it poses no problem at all. And perhaps, if after reading this book you are successful in releasing your child's potential for reading, you will decide to go on to teach him other things as well. Homeschooling is an easier decision to make when you realize it's one you only need to make a year at a time for each individual child.

But even if your child goes to school reading well above second-grade level, his reading ability will not detract from his experience. A good teacher will find outlets for his reading ability, perhaps in reading aloud to the class or helping other children. In this case, be careful not to encourage your child to feel superior to other children, but to think of his early ability as a way to serve.

And if your child is an early reader, rejoice! Early readers show throughout their education a more positive attitude toward learning. Because their first major academic task took place easily, they do not think of learning as a struggle. They are inquisitive and independent. All doors remain open to them.

The Spiritual Side of Reading

We start teaching reading with a spiritual perspective by understanding reading in a different light—not as some invention of man, but as a gift God has given us. It follows naturally from the gift of spoken language. We can rely on the fact that when God has given us a gift, he will help us unwrap it.

Reading is a potential built into each of us just as surely as our potential for spoken language. It is waiting to be released.

Just as the potential for spoken language needs certain environmental factors to be released, so does written language. Teaching reading is not the intimidating, specialized enterprise our culture has made it out to be. It's not pouring knowledge into a child's brain from without. Just as God has predisposed us to share oral communication, he has given us the inner workings we need to share written communication. The ability to read is part of the makeup of your child. Once you understand how it unfolds, you will see that teaching a child to read can be *almost* as easy as watching him learn to speak.

That's why I began with early language development. Usually, no one *has* to study at all to produce a child who speaks first-rate English—as long as he is surrounded by others who speak the same. Exceptions occur, however. In my own case, these were very beneficial.

My eighth child, Jonny, who is fourteen as I write this book, was born with Down syndrome.[5] I know God had a plan when he gave me Jonny. But though this special son would have much to teach me, I had no idea how much more I needed to learn. After twenty-two years with toddlers, I might have thought I was an expert. Raising Jonny has given me so much greater perspective.

That's because children with Down syndrome have most of the same potentials as children with forty-six chromosomes, but they take longer and often need more intervention to be released. Like watching a movie in slow motion, parents with differently-abled children[6] find themselves in a situation where extra attention is focused on each developmental milestone. Instead of asking, "When will he take his first step?" we must ask, "How does the first step happen and what do I need to learn to help him get there?"

In the area of language, with Jonny (and now with the three boys with Down syndrome we've adopted since our ninth child, Madeleine, was born) our family wasn't able to watch the natural progression from cooing to babbling to first words. Instead, we had to initiate and press Jonny toward the goals. Because Down syndrome children's palates and tongues are shaped differently, because of low muscle tone, and because of slower cognitive skills, speech is just more difficult.

Still, most children with Down syndrome nowadays learn to speak and many learn to read. Spending more time and effort at each developmental level with Jonny has given me greater understanding of how each of us is put together.

As I said, children like Jonny are the exception, not the rule. So are children like the ones I taught in the seventies in Washington, DC. As a Montessori teacher in a Head Start funded inner-city preschool, I had three-year-olds entering my class with few or, in some cases, no spoken language skills. These children did not suffer from mental handicaps as Jonny did. They suffered instead from economic and cultural deprivation—living conditions in which they were not surrounded by what they needed to have their gift of speech released. Just a year in a Montessori classroom with teachers and other less-disadvantaged children made a remarkable difference in these children's abilities. Surrounded by the essentials they had been missing at home—mostly just hearing people speak and labeling things like colors and shapes—by the end of the year these children were speaking at levels within the normal range, though noticeably less well than the children whose potential for speech had been released at the appropriate time.

The help these children received through their hours in school, though delayed, was critical to their futures. There is a direct relationship between language and intelligence. As the ability to use language increases, so do cognitive growth and achievement.

The surest way to have an impact on your child's intelligence is to surround him with language and reading.

The Road to Reading

The truth is, even if he's barely walking, you've already started your child on the road to reading. Each day you're teaching him words and connecting those words to the world around him. You've traveled miles of pages reading books together. Nothing instills a love of literature like night after night of *Goodnight Moon* or *Curious George* on a cuddly lap.

If a child has been exposed to books, and especially if he's grown up with adults who enjoy reading, he will need little coaxing to learn how to read.

What he'll need are the tools.

By *tools* I don't mean expensive reading programs. No matter the differences between all of them, the secret those marketers don't want you to know is that there is one key ingredient in the package on which the success of each program depends: your time.

But with the approach I'm about to share with you, you won't have to carve out huge chunks of time to start your child on the path to reading. Most of the work is done before your child ever learns to recognize letters and can be done while you are busy with household chores.

My own years of classroom experience, with children from all economic and ethnic backgrounds, have confirmed that the following tools and techniques work. And in the most casual and comfortable setting possible, I have used this method at home to teach all but the youngest of my twelve children to read.

You Can Do It Too!

You, too, can teach your child to read. Or you can have fun with a few games and techniques that fit easily into the daily routine. No matter how much or how little you do, these early tools will pave the way for your child's later reading skills.

If you are still changing diapers, perhaps you have not thought past potty training. But if your child has developed a vocabulary of fifty or more words—in diapers or out—he is ready.

The Sound Game

The first goal is to make your child aware that words are composed of individual sounds. The Sound Game is guaranteed to get you there. You don't need any special equipment for the Sound Game. Play it in two- to ten-minute snatches anywhere—in the car or doctor's waiting room, while folding the clothes or loading the dishwasher.

The only preparation needed is to brush up on phonetic sounds. Remember to use these rather than the names of letters.

THE PHONETIC ALPHABET

a—as in *apple*	n—as in *nest*
b—as in *bed*	o—as in *ostrich*
c—as in *cat*	p—as in *peanut*
d—as in *daddy*	q—(teach later) as qu (kw)
e—as in *elephant*	r—as in *rabbit*
f—as in *fan*	s—as in *sing*
g—as in *gate*	t—as in *top*
h—as in *hat*	u—as in *up*
i—as in *igloo*	v—as in *victor*
j—as in *jar*	w—as in *wedding*
k—as in *king* (same as c)	x—sounds like *ks,* as in box
l—as in *lemon*	y—as in *yellow*
m—as in *mommy*	z—as in *zebra*

Practice on your own first, isolating each sound. Try to clip the sounds: for instance, *p* sounds like a puff of air, not like *puh.*

For the most part, the consonants are very obvious. But be careful with the vowels. Keep them crisp and clear.

Hear the sounds at www.MommyTeachMe.net 🍎.

What you will be doing is teaching your child—or revealing to him, really—that words are made up of individual sounds. Although some letters have more than one sound, we use only the most common sound for the consonants. And the short sound for the vowels—that is, the sound the vowel most often makes in three-letter words.

When you start, choose familiar sounds, those your child hears frequently in the words he uses. Because they have more emotional appeal and will therefore hold his attention, words about food and people he loves will have more learning impact.

Here's how your first session might go:

Mom: "Let's think of some words that have *mmm* in them—like *m*ilk . . . *m*ommy . . . *m*oon."

Little Sweetie: "Daddy?"

Mom: "I don't hear an *mmm* in 'daddy.' *Mmm* . . . *m*arshmallow . . . *m*erry-go-round."

LS: "Doggy?"

Mom: "*M*ore . . . *m*aybe . . . *m*uffin."

LS: "Cookie?"

Mom: "I don't hear an *mmm* in cookie. Cookie [say it emphasizing the sounds]. *C*—ookie . . . let's think of some words that have *c* [phonetic sound] in them, like *c*ookie . . . *c*ake . . . *c*at."

LS: "Mommy?"

Mom: "*C*ar . . . *c*amel . . . *c*areful."

More likely than not, the first few times you will play this game solo. Your child may offer some words, but they probably will not be the ones you are looking for.

That's OK. Do not correct your child or tell him he is wrong in a direct way. Instead, keep steering him toward the sound, giving as many examples as you can of words that mean a lot to him, as in the example above. Don't forget to use names of family members as well.

In the beginning, you are introducing an idea—that words are made up of individual sounds. As time goes on your child will start to hear this as you keep training his ear to hear the different sounds. You can then use the Sound Game to build vocabulary by using less familiar words.

Remember, this game can be played anywhere, at any time, and for any length of time. It can be interrupted by a phone call or to change the baby's diaper. You don't need to keep a record of any kind.

Keep playing often, and eventually—probably when you least expect it—your child will produce a correct response. Give him a great big hug!

From now on you will be playing the Sound Game with a full-fledged partner. He will offer his own words. Now remember, since we asked for words that have the sound in them, if your child produces a word that does not begin with the sound but does contain it, say the word slowly emphasizing the sound.

More Fun With Sounds

Play *I Spy*—"I spy something that starts with *r*"—then look around the room to name items.

Make a collage of cutout magazine pictures starting with same sound.

Make a small booklet for each sound—one picture per page.

Sort pictures into sounds—all *s* words here, all *m* words there, etc.

Remember also that since *c* and *k* have the same phonetic sound, if you ask for words with *c* and he offers *king*, then that is right. At this point your child does not know anything about letters. Likewise for *s* and soft *c*. Do not correct him as long as the sound is right.

If, after initially catching on, your child makes a mistake now and then, avoid the words *no* and *wrong*. Simply steer him in the right direction, as follows:

"Do you hear a *p* in tiger? *T . . . i . . . g . . . r*? [Shake head] You don't hear it? Do you hear a *p* in *pop*corn?"

Children like the Sound Game. Just as a child enjoys pulling apart the petals of a flower to see how it is put together, once his attention is drawn to the fact that his language is made up of sounds, he will become interested enough to explore on his own.

Eventually, you may find your child playing on his own. Once you are sure he grasps the concept of individual sounds and can hear them clearly—even if you have not gone over every sound in the alphabet—he is ready for the Letter Game.

Sesame Street

From its earliest days I have been very fond of a certain children's television show. I saw the premier thirty years ago when my oldest daughter, Samantha, was eighteen months old. I remember how thrilled both of us were that she now had a show just for her, a show that would teach her in a uniquely fun-filled format. The show provided a break for me to cook dinner (although as a more experienced mother now, I'd say get your child working in the kitchen with you), but I often found myself standing at the kitchen door, mesmerized by the action on Sesame Street.

I found enough value in Sesame Street that even during our fifteen years without TV, we used a monitor and VCR for the children to watch tapes our friends made for us.

For thirty years Sesame Street has delivered little disappointment. By exemplifying everyday harmony among races, the show has made a tremendous contribution to children's understanding and acceptance of cultural differences. Sesame Street was one of the very first television shows to incorporate children and adults with disabilities (I still get a thrill every time I see the little girl with Down syndrome. Jonny is madly in love with her), including a regular who is deaf and uses sign language. But even on the more subtle level of working out difficulties caused by those whose personalities clash (like Oscar and just about anyone) or who seem too slow (Mr. Snuffleupagus) or too air-headed (Big Bird), Sesame Street excels in championing kindness and tolerance.

The shows are always lively and unpredictable, full of tantalizing tidbits of information—such as what happens to garbage and how peanut butter is made. They teach urban children what life is like on a farm and farm children what life is like in the city (sugar-coated, of course, but still much more bustling).

The characters are colorful and well textured (green and scaly, blue and clumpy, yellow and feathery) and absolutely full of human foibles and charm. Most everyone I know has a personal favorite. In fact, I've often wondered if someone could devise a personality test from who your favorite Sesame Street character is.

Many parents reading this book grew up on Sesame Street themselves.

One of the teaching techniques Sesame Street popularized was sound-bite education. If you grew up on it, you know what I mean: Present a compelling image for a brief time, make it memorable, then move on. What a fun way to learn! And though the downside may be a shorter attention span, the show was enormously successful in imparting information to children, particularly in teaching children their alphabet.

But, oh, how I wish they had taught those letters differently!

The Sounds vs. Letter Names

Would it surprise you to know that the child who knows all twenty-six letters by name is really no closer to reading than the one who knows none at all? If so, then read on. Once you've seen how the phonetic approach to reading works, you'll understand completely. You'll see why—despite my admiration for Sesame Street—if I had my druthers, I'd rewrite the way they teach the alphabet.

Knowing the names of letters does not facilitate reading at all; it may even make it more difficult. A child can look at a word and say, "dee – oh – gee" from breakfast to dinner and never have a clue that those letters spell the word *dog*. However, if he has learned the phonetic sounds for the letters rather than their names, he will string the sounds together easily to form a word with which he is familiar. What a joyful discovery! How easy that makes his way into the world of reading.

That's why practice with phonetic sounds must come before the child even sees the letters that represent them.

Many methods of teaching reading bypass this important step. They do not follow the natural learning patterns of preschoolers (which may be why, as I pointed out earlier, some educators don't understand that it is actually very appropriate to teach reading to preschoolers). Often, when adults set out to teach children to read, they do so in a way that would be best for another adult.

Children learn differently from adults. Their minds are not yet developmentally equipped to handle abstract concepts without having found their footing on the concrete. That is, you can tell them from now until the proverbial cows come home what a real cow looks like, but until they see a cow, they will not really be able to "see" it in their minds.

Likewise, giving children the names of letters along with the symbols gives them no solid foundation of what those letters really are, what they stand for, what they mean. They remain merely empty symbols.

In the *Mommy, Teach Me!* approach, much time is spent pouring the foundation for reading. It is simple, inexpensive, and exceedingly easy to do. So easy that if you have been playing the Sound Game with your child, you may not realize that you have already done it!

The true foundation for reading is in sound recognition. Through the Sound Game, the child comes to realize that our language is not only composed of words, but that each word is composed of individual sounds. His ear becomes trained to hear those sounds—in the many different combinations and patterns.

This is the concrete, the reality that the child needs to be on friendly terms with—before he even comes in contact with letters. Having given your child the experience of hearing all the sounds that make up the words he uses, you can now give him the symbol. Only now it will be more than a symbol because he will know what it means. Once a child has familiarity with the concrete, he has something to which he can attach the abstract symbol, like a ribbon that keeps the balloon from flying away.

The Letter Game

Once you've become a pro at the Sound Game—learning all the sounds, isolating them for your child, and making him aware that they are parts of words—you have already become a qualified teacher of phonetics. You have laid all the groundwork necessary for the next step: introducing your child to the letters that serve as symbols for those sounds.

Letters to Touch and Teach

The only equipment you will need to play the Letter Game with your child is a set of lowercase letters.

Sandpaper letters offer a multisensory approach to learning phonetic sounds and letter formation.

Do not even consider using uppercase letters at this point with your child. Think about it. Look at the book you have in your hands. How many letters are on this page? And how many are capitals? Not too many.

Capitals come into play only when the child begins to read books and construct sentences himself, and by then he'll be so secure in his reading that he will simply absorb them as he goes along. At this beginning stage, however, capitals are a distraction from the real work at hand. Knowing them will not help your child read.

Find a set of lowercase letters large enough for your child to trace with his fingers. Classic Montessori uses sandpaper letters on coated particleboard, which are beautiful but expensive. Fortunately, these are easily replicable with sandpaper, scissors, rubber cement, and heavy cardboard—plus the directions in appendix G and the letter templates at 🍎. There are also good, not-so-expensive replicas of the official Montessori sandpaper letters available online or from teacher supply stores.

Though sandpaper letters are not essential to the *Mommy, Teach Me!* approach, they are well worth making (especially if you have or plan to have more children) because they are quite effective for teaching our little concrete thinkers. As you will see, we will not just be showing the letter to the child and giving its phonetic sound, we will be asking him to trace it and say it at the same time—practice for future writing skills. Studies have shown that the more senses engaged in any learning process, the more efficient the learning and the longer the retention. That's why adults use audiovisuals instead of just telling, and why we take notes instead of just listening.

This is even truer with children: the more senses involved with learning letter-sound correspondence, the more readily children absorb the knowledge. The sandpaper letters have the distinct advantage of offering a textured surface for little fingers to trace, thereby engaging not only sight and hearing but also giving back some very tactile feedback.

But if you don't have the time or budget, if you're in a hurry, or you just plain want to keep things simple, just go to your local toy store and buy a set of magnetic letters—lowercase only—and stick them on the refrigerator door. Let your child play with them for a few days.

And don't feel guilty about it—whatever you decide.

Correct Letter Formation

While you are on the path to reading, you will also be preparing your child for writing. Another benefit of the multisensory approach is that you will not only be teaching your child to recognize the letters visually, but also to trace its shape with his fingers. Get him off to the best start possible. If you need to, brush up on correct letter formation in appendix H.

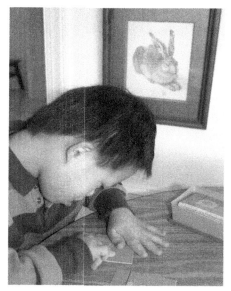

Letters in Groups of Three

Teach your child letters in groups of three—three will provide more interest than one or two but will not be too

Teach your child how to trace the letters while he says the sounds.

overwhelming for your child to learn at one time. The groups are selected with the following factors in mind:

- contrast in phonetic sound,

- contrast in appearance of letter, and

- usability in phonetic word formation (a phonetic word is one in which every letter says its true phonetic sound).

The first two contrasts will make it easier for your child to learn the letters. If you were trying to teach *f* and *v* in the same lesson (similar phonetic sounds) or *j* and *i* (similar appearance) your child would have more room for confusion. Make it easier for your child to learn by maximizing the contrast between the shapes and sounds.

The third factor—usability in word formation—though not as critical to the child's success, simply means your child will be off and running sooner. As you will see, even before he knows all the letters, you will be encouraging him in the Word Game to make words of the letters he knows. So make sure the letters you choose will go a long way, and introduce vowels early.

Teaching Technique

In the Three Period Lesson, Maria Montessori devised a method to teach letters, numbers, shapes, and colors—any kind of vocabulary—to children in a way that would maximize their chances of success. It is a highly effective technique for any parent who would like to extend a child's vocabulary through the use of nature cards.

SUGGESTED SEQUENCE FOR TEACHING LETTERS

For teaching letters, three letter groups are optimum.
Here is the order I have used for years:

m, a, t

s, i, p

c, r, j

n, o, g

f, u, d

b, e, w

v, l, x

h, y, z

However, once you have taught your child the first three or four groups, he will be absorbing new letters easily in the Word Game, so they will no longer *have* to be taught in any particular order.

THREE PERIOD LESSON

First Period: *Naming*—teacher presents and names three objects, one after another.

Second Period: *Practice*—teacher provides name, child chooses matching object.

Third Period: *Testing*—teacher asks child to name the object.

The Three Period Lesson is perfect for teaching letters. Just keep in mind that the first two periods require the greatest amount of time. Don't even go to the third period until you know it will only take a minute because your child is sure to succeed.

First Period: Naming—"This is *m*."

Sit to the left of your child with the three letters face down (or if using something like magnetic letters, under a napkin).

Play the Sound Game briefly: "Let's think of some words with *m* in them: mommy . . . mister . . . mountain." This is familiar territory. You have prepared your child, and at this point he knows what the game is about. After he contributes a few words, ask your child, with some drama, "Do you want to see what *m* looks like?"

This is the key question and the key moment. Your child has the concrete knowledge of the letter through its sound. Now for the first time you are telling him the letter is also something visual. What child wouldn't say yes?

Place the letter—almost with an attitude of reverence—on the table or the floor in front of you (you should both be seeing the letter right side up and you should be on your child's left. Even if you are left-handed—unless you suspect your child is also—always teach letters from this right-handed position).

What About Lefties?

The days when adults forced children into right-handedness are long gone. Most children show a clear preference for right-handedness, but others tend to show early ambidexterity—the use of both hands. In this case, since being left-handed does impose a little extra difficulty, we do offer objects to children from a position that encourages them to develop right-handedness—unless the child himself has shown a clear preference for the left.

If you do have a lefty, you will need to rethink everything you do with your child to make it work for him (see appendix I).

If you are using sandpaper letters or something similar, place one on the table and turn it at an angle as you would a piece of paper you were about to write on (the bottom left-hand corner should be pointing at you). Hold the board down with your left hand, as you would hold a piece of paper when writing. Here you are implanting an idea of correct writing posture.

Now slowly and attentively trace the letter with your index and middle fingers held together, as though you were writing the letter—with the proper form.

Let natural lefties trace with left hand—see Appendix I.

Watch your own fingers. Your child will too. As you come to the end of the letter, say its sound: "*m.*" (Notice the interplay of the senses: visual, auditory, and tactile.)

Repeat until you think your child can do it himself, then invite him to trace, holding the letter at a slant with his left hand as though he were writing on paper and tracing with right index and middle fingers. If your child is very young or his hand unsure, you may guide his hand smoothly over the letter. Say the sound with him at the end.

Convey a feeling of immense satisfaction—*Wow, here is what it looks like!* It may be old hat to us, but what a revelation to the mind of a child!

Invite your child to repeat the tracing and sound as many times as he likes. Do not hurry him.

When you feel a connection has been firmly established, put the first letter aside and start with the next: "Let's think of some words with *a* in them: *a*pple . . . *a*stronaut . . . *a*ctor."

Repeat this process until all three letters have been thoroughly introduced.

Second Period: Practicing—"Find *m* and trace it."

Once you have introduced each of the three letters, review them quickly, still using only the phonetic sound:

"Here is *m*." (Put it down on the table face up.)

"Here is *a*." (Put it down on the table face up.)

"Here is *t*." (Put it down on the table face up.)

"Now I'm going to mix them all up." (Make a big show of shuffling.)

"Now, can you find *t* and trace it?"

"Please put *a* on the shelf."

"I'll close my eyes and you can put *m* in my hands."

If you have more than one child, this part can be very lively. Here your child will get a lot of practice matching the sound and the symbol.

The secret here is that you are not asking your child to tell you the sound, but are providing the new information and asking him to match it with what he knew to begin with. This makes it an easier task—like the difference between a matching quiz and an open-ended question test. In the second period, because you are supplying the sound, it is easier for your child to succeed. Keep on practicing until you are sure he knows which letter is which. Only when you are sure he's sure should you go on to the third period.

Third Period: Testing—"Trace this and tell me what it says."

Once you are sure your child knows the letters, make a show of mixing them up again, then place one in front of him and ask, "Trace this and tell me what it says."

Notice tracing is involved in all three periods. The idea of tracing as much as possible is important for the reasons shared before:

- to help the child retain and

- to prepare the hand for writing letters later on.

If your child does make a mistake, simply remind him of the correct sound and go on. If, despite a long second period, he seems not to remember the sounds well at all, don't scold. Remember, he's got a long time to learn to read. Simply put the letters away together and repeat the lesson the next day.

Once your child has learned the first three letters, you can put them away until the next lesson—hopefully (though not always possible) the next day. At your second lesson, review the first three letters before introducing the next three. If your child remembers only two, you may substitute the one he has forgotten for one of the new ones, keeping in mind the guidelines for contrast in appearance and sound. Or you may pick it up again later.

If you have a lot on your mind, you may want to keep a list of which letters you've introduced and which your child has made his own through memory.

The Word Game

Once he knows eight to ten letters, your child is ready to start forming words. Teaching the entire alphabet of sounds and letters—that is, completing the Sound Game and the Letter Game before starting the Word Game—is not only unnecessary but would probably be counterproductive.

So don't wait. Keep the momentum going by introducing the Word Game as soon as your child knows two vowels and six consonants. This new extension of his knowledge will become a powerful incentive in itself. Your child will pick up letters easily as you continue making words together.

With the Word Game, you will be helping your child spell words through breaking them down into component sounds. This is not yet reading, but the most accessible path into reading for the young child. This approach makes the way smooth for reading because it is built on the child's need to start with the concrete, adding the abstract after.

As you help your child form words, he will be hearing and saying the concrete sounds, then finding the abstract symbol. This is much easier for him than looking at letters put together by someone else and trying to abstract the word from them.

You will notice with the Word Game, the child actually "writes" before reading. But since his own motor skills are probably not ready, instead of using a pencil, he will be manipulating a set of letters to put together three-letter phonetic words.

In the meantime, you can help your child perfect his fine-motor skills through exercises I describe in detail in *Mommy, Teach Me!*

FINGER FITNESS—GETTING READY TO WRITE

Your child has been getting ready to write since the first Cheerio he picked up between his finger and thumb. Pincer grasp is the key, so anything you give him to help develop that skill will help:

- puzzles with knobs
- tweezers
- sorting small objects
- coloring books (staying in the lines is a great exercise in control)

Now's the time to purchase a set of magnetic letters. Search for a set with only lowercase letters (of course!) and stick several of each one your child knows on the refrigerator door. No need to have a formal setup for the Word Game, unless you want to. And there's a distinct advantage to having them on the refrigerator door: although at first you will need to stick close to the letters yourself as you guide your child through the Word Game, later as your child becomes more independent in forming words himself, you will be able to suggest words to him as you stir the spaghetti or empty the dishwasher.

MORE FUN WITH LETTERS—EXTENSION EXERCISES

- Trace letters in a box of damp sand, in cool whip, pudding, or peanut butter.
- Trace letters in the air with big movements.

It's actually better to wait until your child has developed some control before giving him paper and pencil to write his own letters. That way he has a greater chance of success. And you know how much more inclined we are ourselves when we see a little success!

First Lesson

Gather the letters your child knows, plus one or two new ones. You should be able to make many three-letter phonetic words from them. (The words must be truly phonetic: that is, the letters must stand only for the sounds you have taught.)

Show your child the letters one by one, reviewing the sounds, then placing them on the left side of the refrigerator door (or whatever surface you are working on). Sit on the left side of your child and say:

"Let's make some words. How about 'cat'? *c . . . a . . . t.*"

Break the word down into component sounds.

"Where is *c*?"

Make a show of looking for the right letter and offering it for his agreement. Then place the letter to the right of the scattered letters at the top left of what will become a column of words.

"*c . . . a . . .*"

As you say *c*, point to it; as you say *a*, point to the space to the right of it. Find the *a* and place it.

"c . . . a . . . t"

Again, point to the sounds as you say them, then the empty space. Find the *t* and place it. Now point to the letters as you say the sounds, several times, each time bringing the sounds closer together. If you have been conscientious about clipping the consonants (saying *c* crisply rather than "cuh"), they will glide together.

"C . . . a . . . t . . . c . . . a . . . t . . . cat"

---

75 THREE-LETTER PHONETIC WORDS

(There are many more!)

cat	mop	jam	sit	wet
mom	dad	map	can	sip
fat	run	jog	zip	jet
ram	dog	cob	web	pop
cap	rat	bug	hat	lip
rip	jet	gun	hop	hen
pet	bag	yes	hug	hot
rug	let	tub	bag	rub
log	fit	sis	ask	yes
bib	mix	lot	win	jug
men	bit	mob	cab	peg
pig	tax	fun	nod	hum
wag	fix	can	wed	got
lag	did	gum	red	tip
vet	wig	peg	tan	lab

"Now let's make 'jam' . . . *j* . . . *a* . . . *m*—*j* . . . *j* . . ."

If *j* is one of the letters your child hasn't learned yet, introduce it:

"This is *j*."

Place it under the *c* as the beginning of the next word on the list you will be making. Go on to finish the word in the same manner as before, reviewing and blending the sounds when complete.

When you feel he is ready, let your child take over finding and placing the letters. Make a list of as many words as you have time for. When you are finished, say something like this:

"Are we finished? OK, let's go back over the words together."

Now, starting at the top of the list, go back over the words, pointing to the letters and sounding each of them, then blending them together to form the word:

"*c* . . . *a* . . . *t*—*cat*."

As you go over the list, point to the letters as you say them and then glide your finger left to right under the letters as you read the word. This left-to-right movement and reading the list from top to bottom is preparation for reading.

Do not ask your child to read the words himself. It is important to make sure a child can succeed before asking him to do something. At this point, a child cannot read.

Over the days and weeks to come, as you play the Word Game, you will see your child becoming more independent. You will be able to tell him a word and he will sound it out with less and less help from you. Then it's easy to get a lot of practice because you can give him words no matter how busy you are. Do try to go over his list with him at the end though.

Eventually, he can do the Word Game independently.

Keep introducing new letters. As your child begins to work more independently, you may slip in a new letter or two and ask him next time to find the ones he doesn't know yet, then give him the sounds. Remember to keep the words phonetic.

When your child is ready, you can progress (in increasing level of difficulty) to two-syllable words made of three-letter phonetic parts, then four-letter words and finally five-letter words:

TWO-SYLLABLE WORDS MADE OF THREE-LETTER PHONETIC PARTS

magnet	picnic	cobweb	zigzag
basket	pigpen	napkin	sunset

More at 🍎.

50 FOUR-LETTER PHONETIC WORDS

milk	jump	skip	camp	glad
lamp	went	last	wind	club
mend	bent	grab	list	flag
dent	sand	past	brim	clip
damp	lost	spot	tent	plug
rent	flap	west	stop	rust
plan	crop	stem	trip	just
snap	tank	drum	frog	plum
trim	snug	crib	slam	scat
swim	twig	grin	drop	flap

More at 🍎.

25 FIVE-LETTER PHONETIC WORDS

plant	stamp	split	blast	stand
frost	clamp	brisk	scant	twist
grasp	split	scrap	scrub	drift
scram	strip	stung	blend	strum
trust	strap	swung	draft	prong

More at 🍎.

At some point, possibly even while your child is still working on three-letter words, you will notice that he is starting to sound out the words completely on his own. You might say "man" and with little hesitation he will say, "*m . . . a . . . n.*"

In this case, don't wait for him to go to four letters or five letters. As soon as you hear this, you know your child is ready to read.

Ready to Read

The Phonetic Object Game

For your child's first adventure in reading, you will need a basket with five or six small phonetic items you've collected—for instance, a nut, a jet, a pig, a dog, a cat. You will also need slips of paper and a pencil.

COLLECTIBLES FOR EARLY READING

Start a collection of *phonetic* objects—small charms or models that can be used for labeling:

pig	jet	nut	dog	cat
frog	can	pin	peg	bell
bug	lid	top	lock	gum
doll	plug	cap	tack	cup

Collect *nonphonetic* objects for the next stage. Once your child is comfortable, start introducing these, one at a time, each time he does the Object Game:

fish	spool	penny	dime	jeep
nail	football	boat	shell	lace
soap	chick	fly	spoon	cube
knot	key	flower	bird	bowl

These are just examples, of course. You will find more at 🍎. Once you start, you will find yourself building quite a collection. Your children will love labeling these objects.

For his first introduction to the Phonetic Object Game, sitting on your child's left, remove all the objects from the basket, naming each as you place it on the table. Now, as your child watches, print the name of one object slowly and carefully on a slip of paper. Hand the paper to your child and ask, "Can you find this for me?"

Give your child a chance to sound out the word for himself, but if he needs prompting, get him started with the sounds. He should find the object and place the label next to it.

The key to your child's success here is all the preparation that has come before, plus the limited field of objects from which to choose. He may or may not need a little help, but he should be able to label the objects. Keep the labels in the basket for him to practice, and as days go by, slip in more objects with corresponding labels.

Using stamps to "write" words.

The Phonetic Object Game works as a transition because it is based on attaching the name to something concrete. But it is just a bridge. As your child gains confidence—"Hey, I can read this one, Mommy!"—he will be able to move easily into the abstract, reading flash cards you make or buy. Use the same sequence as you did with the Word Game:

- three-letter phonetic words,

- two-syllable words made of two three-letter phonetic syllables,

- four-letter phonetic words, and

- five-letter phonetic words.

BLENDS

As you move from three-letter to four- and five-letter words, you will encounter what professionals call "blends." A blend is simply two consonants together—for example, *st, sp, sc, br, bl, mp, nt, nd*—which retain their phonetic sound, but which a beginning reader may need a little extra help with. If your child needs extra reinforcement, you can make a set of cards, each with a list of words with a particular blend, similar to the diagraph cards discussed in the following section.

DIAGRAPHS

A greater challenge is presented by nonphonetic combinations called diagraphs. A diagraph is a double consonant (two consonants together) or a vowel and consonant combination pronounced as a single sound.

These can be introduced quite simply once your child has mastered the Phonetic Object Game by introducing nonphonetic combinations—for instance, a fish. Help him sound out the word by saying, "Oh, this is something you need to remember: when *s* and *h* are together, they always say *sh*."

Or in other combinations:

"When you see *ck* together, they just say *c*."

"When two *e*'s are together, they say *ee*."

You may reinforce these common nonphonetic combinations (though with many children you will never need to) with five-by-seven-inch index cards with lists of words having the same diagraph:

SAMPLE DIAGRAPH CARDS

ee	oo	i_e	a_e	ai
feet	moon	mine	late	pail
see	soon	tire	same	rain
week	tool	hide	tale	maid
teen	scoot	file	wade	fair
keep	balloon	bite	fake	nail
reed	raccoon	hive	pane	wait
peel	boot	wife	maze	waist

ay	ch	y	y	o_e
say	chip	baby	cry	hole
day	chest	penny	sky	poke
may	chop	bunny	try	rope
play	chug	skinny	fry	home
stay	inch	funny	my	dome
way	chick	silly	fly	note
ray	bench	holy	empty	vote

One combination per card. Use red markers to write the combinations, black for the other letters. Other nonphonetic combinations include *th* (two sounds, as in this and breath), *ow* (two sounds, as in bowl and owl), *qu, ou, oi, oy, kn, gn*. Keep in mind that for most readers, you will not need to make a card for every sound. For the best readers, you will not need cards at all—they will learn the exceptions as they read.

When you introduce a card to your child, explain, saying for example,

"When you see two *o*'s together, they say *oo*."

Then just go over the words one by one, helping him read *oo* instead of *o . . . o.*

PUZZLE WORDS

Create a set of Puzzle Words for your child. Old business cards are the perfect size (and price!), plus it's easy to wrap a rubber band around them. On the back of each, print a word that has no logical reason to be spelled the way it is, but is essential to our vocabulary.

PUZZLE WORDS		
you	I	are
our	the	why
eye	oh	sew
have	some	busy
what	one	two
once	come	done
both	they	were
was	four	put

These are just some examples. There are plenty more! You can find templates at 🍎 to print, cut, and laminate your own set.

Puzzle words must be taught by sight. You might explain:

"There are some words we just can't sound out. We just have to know them when we see them."

Teach puzzle words in groups of three, using the three-period lesson format. Pop them in your purse on your way to the pediatrician's office or any place you'll have a couple minutes to sit with no laundry or dishes to do. Then you can use them like flash cards with your child to make your waiting time worthwhile.

Let It Flow

But hold on to your hat—don't get carried away with the exceptions. The powerful spark ignited when your child makes his first reading breakthrough (as with the Phonetic Object Game, the first time he "gets" it) will amaze and humble you as your child "explodes" into reading.

Think of how your child learned to speak: starting with only a few words, somewhere between two and three he exploded into full language. You didn't have to teach him every word or proper sentence structure. God built that capacity for speech development into him.

God also built the capacity to communicate through the written word into him. During the preschool years, once a child succeeds at reading phonetically, with very little help he will explode into reading, picking up books and enjoying the challenge of figuring out new words himself. Just as much as your child wanted to communicate through his own spoken words, he will want to read the words in all those wonderful books you have provided and have read to him.

Because of your child's motivation, you will not need to teach him every rule and every exception to perfect his reading skills. Just as he learned to speak through exposure to spoken language, he will learn to read through exposure to books.

Now the greatest part of your work is over (and it really didn't seem that much like work did it, after all?).

You have prepared your child well. The rest of the work will be his. In the next chapter I will share more ways to exercise his reading skills. But believe me, your child will be having so much fun, it will never seem like work at all.

Remember: a well-prepared child has confidence, and the thrill of being able to read is a powerful motivator. At this stage, you will have to do little coaxing. Once you initiate a young child into reading, he will usually take over the controls himself.

Reading Tips

If you've read board books to your baby, then left them in easy reach, you've already discovered books have great drawing power even for little ones. The beauty of the board books is that toddlers can be trusted to use them independently.

At the age of two or three, you should be able to trust your child with other books—the kind with paper pages—as well. The key is to prepare him carefully by instilling a high regard for reading and a reverence for books.

I mentioned before the importance of your child seeing you read. In addition to reading to him, find times to read side-by-side—you engrossed in your book while he "reads" his. Make it a habit to take children's books with you everywhere—to the doctor's office, the beach or grandma's, on the bus, short trips or vacation. Read in the morning, before naps, after dinner, before bed. Be careful never to make it seem like a chore; treat it like a refreshing break, something you look forward to wholeheartedly.

Take trips to the library and the bookstore. When you've watched a movie that originated as a book, check the book out of the library. Your child will be impressed to know a video he loves began as a book.

Make sure your child sees the practical application of reading all around: point out highway signs, labels on cereal boxes, maps, newspapers, telephone directories, cookbooks. When the mail comes, read the name and address on the envelope to show him who it's for and who it's from. Read the mail to him. Emphasize that this is an important way we have to *communicate*.

Have lots of books in the house as well as snuggly places to read. Make your child's solo reading extra special by creating a reading nook. It doesn't require much area—after all, a child isn't very big!—a cozy chair or maybe just a large comfy pillow on the floor next to a sunny window. Decorate with some small pictures hung at his level. Place an inexpensive bookcase (or cover sturdy boxes with contact paper to make your own) to hold his own books.

Begin early to teach your child how to handle books with respect. (If you grew up in a home where books were used for coasters, you might want to rethink this now that you're paying for them yourself!) When you read with your child, exaggerate the care with which you turn the pages. Teach your child when he is finished reading a book to place it upright on the shelf with the binding facing out.

A reading nook invites a child to snuggle up with books.

Teach your child to turn pages carefully.

As You Read

Start a book by reading the title and the author with your child. This lets him know that a book is someone's creation. You might want to talk about the cover art and mention the name of the artist. This lets him know that a book is a collaborative effort.

Start early to help your child make the distinction between reality and fantasy. There are three kinds of books:

- stories that really happened (the Bible, historical accounts),

- stories that could happen (as in *Ira Sleeps Over*—a dilemma any child could face), and

- stories that could never happen at all (*Where the Wild Things Are*).

Some people question using fantasy at all with children. Montessori did; she felt that toddlers—because they could not think abstractly—could not distinguish between fantasy and reality. Besides, she reasoned, reality is so full of marvelous things, we could easily fill the early years just teaching all the wonders of the world, saving fantasy for later.

Likewise, some parents, for religious reasons, wish to avoid fantasy, or even stories that have animals as characters.

I see value in fantasy, although it requires an extra amount of discernment on the part of parents to make sure the author's message (because every author has one) is compatible with what they want their children to learn. Books with animal characters—I especially think of Russell Hoban's *Frances* books—can teach important lessons in charming and nonthreatening ways. Through projecting the child's conflicts and fears—for instance, the birth of a sibling—onto something safe (like a whimsical raccoon), the author helps children cope. Books like *Where the Wild Things Are*, which some Christian parents might reject, deal with very real and inexpressible childhood feelings, showing them resolved and security restored at the end.

Remember, at this age a child cannot think abstractly. Therefore the only way you can teach him about courage, loyalty, faith, and love is through stories.

Christian parents can get more out of books that are not specifically Christian through discussion in which they explore Christian themes. That way you are teaching your children that spirituality does not exist in vacuum. It's not tied to specific times and books. It's a filter through which they can view any information that comes their way. As C. S. Lewis wrote: "I believe in Christianity as I believe that the sun has risen. Not only because I see it, but because I see everything by it."[7] You don't have to limit your child's reading to self-defined "Christian" books, nor would you want to if you want to produce a good reader. The classics are the classics because they have stood the test of time; most of them are not overtly Christian, yet they are full of Christian themes. Keep these principles in mind as

Reading to a sibling builds relationship.

your reader matures, and you will definitely see the results: a well-rounded child whose faith is not compartmentalized but is influenced by everything he reads because that's what you've taught him.

Whatever you are reading, it helps to know there are really three ways to read a book:

- Comprehensively—spending time on each page to discuss and ask questions.

- Technically—noting sentences, words, letters ("Do you see an *s* on this page?").

- Dramatically—presenting material uninterruptedly, with focus only on the story, holding any questions or comments until the end.

It's a good idea to do some of each, though the first and third are where you'll spend the most time.

Above all, have a good time! Reading with your child can be so freeing, especially if you've always wanted to be a little less reserved! Now's the time to be dramatic: any parent can be Oscar-worthy in the eyes of an admiring child. Make stories come alive through variations in tempo, pitch, or inflection. Create character voices, make background noises, use hands and arms to illustrate emotions.

Since you will be reading stories more than once (I once figured out I'd read *Go, Dog, Go* at least six hundred times), you might as well make them as enjoyable as you can for yourself!

Reading to a younger sibling builds confidence.

Book Recommendations
Two to Five Years

(Again, though there are newer editions of these books available, I have used the original year of publication to provide some idea of the timelessness and staying-power of children's books that have become classics.)

Read-Aloud Stories

Bedtime For Frances (also *A Baby Sister for Frances, A Birthday for Frances,* etc.), Russell Hoban, HarperCollins, 1960.

You will surely fall in love with Frances, the raccoon who brings the problems of childhood to life in such a warm and whimsical way. Frances's mother and father are always there to help her through her latest crisis, with serenity and a sense of humor.

The Bible Illustrated for Little Children, Ella K. Lindvall, Moody Press, 1985.

Walk through the Bible with your child—from creation to Paul's imprisonment—with these gorgeously-illustrated, captivatingly-told, one-page stories. Each story is followed by conversational questions.

The Carrot Seed, Ruth Krauss, Trophy Press, 1945.

A little boy plants a seed and, though he receives a lot of discouragement, does all he can to help it grow. His efforts are rewarded.

Cat in the Hat (also *Fox in Socks* and *Green Eggs and Ham*), Dr. Seuss, Random House, 1957.

One of the best parts of being a parent is getting to revisit old favorites like these. These funny, fantastic books beg to be read over and over. Later, because they are as close as best friends, they will become confidence-builders as your child begins to read.

Corduroy, Don Freeman, Viking, 1968.

A stuffed bear wants a home, but waiting in the department store has taken its toll. Still, a little girl falls in love with him. A tale about security and unconditional love.

Giant Steps for Little People, Kenneth N. Taylor, Tyndale, 1985.

The Sermon on the Mount and the Ten Commandments broken into "bite-sized morsels a very young child can grasp and grow on." Each page offers a spiritual truth, a practical application (with lots of opportunities for parent/child conversation), a prayer, and a memory verse. A treasure.

Go, Dog, Go, Philip D. Eastman, Random House, 1961.

One of the silliest teaching books around, this book is jam-packed with adjectives and prepositions—important for later skills—but is still guaranteed to give your child a fun time. Another book that will eventually double as an early reader.

Ira Sleeps Over, Bernard Waber, Houghton Mifflin Co., 1973.

How exciting to be invited to spend the night at a friend's house—but how scary to face the prospect of sleeping without your teddy bear! A childhood dilemma depicted with empathy and humor.

Just in Case You Ever Wonder, Max Lucado, Word, 1992.

A sort of "have I told you lately that I love you?" from parent to child, this tender book will build your child's sense of peace and protection. A reminder that you are always there for him—and so is God.

The Little Engine That Could, Watty Piper, Platt & Munck, 1930.

A wonderful message for children: with a humble heart and a little determination, even the smallest can save the day. A classic for generations.

The Little Red Hen, various authors and publishers since 1942.

Hooray for a good work ethic! The little red hen asks for but receives no help in her efforts to put bread on the table. Yet all who wouldn't help would like to eat. In a refreshingly old-fashioned triumph of moral consequences, they don't get to.

Madeline, Ludwig Bemelmans, Viking, 1958.

A classic told in charming rhyme, this book opens the window to a different world, where little French girls go to boarding school and one has her appendix removed.

Make Way for Ducklings, Robert McCloskey, Viking, 1941.

Such a family-values story! Mr. and Mrs. Mallard search for the perfect spot to raise their family, with some assistance from a friendly police officer. Told and illustrated with humor and warmth.

Millions of Cats, Wanda Gag, various publishers since 1928.

An enchanting tale of a man who comes home with "hundreds of cats, thousands of cats, millions and billions and trillions of cats." Lots of rhythm, rhyme, and repetition make a strong point—humility can keep you from harm, and love can bring out beauty.

My Very First Book of Bible Words, Mary Hollingsworth, Honor Kidz, 2003.

A child's faith vocabulary: words like *worship, obey, family,* and *church* are illustrated and made real through brief definitions, Bible quotes, and activities.

Noah's Ark, Peter Spier, Doubleday, 1977.

This award-winning version is accompanied by sparkling, intricate, and highly satisfying illustrations. Not much accompanying text, but recommended for stimulating imagination and discussion.

Peter's Chair, Ezra Jack Keats, Trophy Press, 1967.

Peter faces life with a new sister—including all his furniture being painted pink. How will he learn to accept his new place in the family?

Play with Me, Marie Hall Ets, Viking, 1955.

On my first read of this book, I found it a little too quiet—but that's the point. Children must get the message, because they seem fascinated by this tale of a lonely girl who finds friends in the forest through cultivating patience and stillness. After reading, challenge your child to be still and quiet—a great lesson in self-control.

The Puppy Who Wanted a Boy, Jane Thayer, Scholastic, 1968.

Petey the puppy wants a boy for Christmas, but his mother tells him he'll have to find one on his own. Of course there's a happy ending!

The Rainbow Fish, Marcus Pfister, Scholastic, 1992.

A new tale destined to become a classic: the story of a beautiful, proud, and selfish little fish who discovers life isn't much fun without sharing. A finely drawn message just right for children. The editions with real glittery scales shimmer too!

Stone Soup, Ann McGovern, Scholastic, 1968.

The hilarious tale of an old woman and the clever vagabond who convinces her that she can make soup from a stone, while persuading her to add a little of this and a little of that. Children love this story—and then making soup afterward.

Where the Wild Things Are, Maurice Sendak, Harper and Row, 1963.

The wildly imaginative tale of a boy sent to his room with no supper who finds his way through an emotional jungle filled with funny-looking monsters—then back to his own room. Reaffirms the old notion—there's just no place like home!

*** Check 🍎 for expanded list.***

CHAPTER
3
Exploring Language:
Five to Seven Years

ONCE YOUR CHILD BEGINS TO READ, especially when he's learned in a natural manner appropriate to his age level, his reading will continue to improve with little effort on your part—as long as he continues to read.

Soon he will be ready to read books. But you can provide a stronger foundation for him if you spend just a little more time building his confidence and his skills.

Strengthening Early Ready Skills

Recognizing Words

Your child enjoyed the Phonetic Object Game, labeling a basket full of objects. As his word-attack skills increase, motivate him with labels for everything in sight: window, door, chair, couch, sink.

If you want to invest a little more time and effort, scout out the hardware department for organizers with little plastic drawers. Then label a drawer for every room in your house and fill each drawer with labels for the contents of that particular room.

Write action words on slips of paper and have your child read and perform the action: hop, skip, walk, run, twirl, dance, glide, slide, spin, shuffle, bounce, dart, zoom, march, roll, strut, plod, trudge, flit, race. This can be a vocabulary builder too!

If you are reading a magazine or book that is too advanced for his reading level, challenge him to find words on the page that he knows. Look for words he knows on labels, on the highway, and in the mail.

Understanding What Words Do

At the same time, keep increasing his awareness of how words are used in our language. From labeling, he knows that some words name things. Although the child isn't ready for the abstract concept of "parts of speech," his early work in labeling things in his environment will lay the groundwork for his learning later on that nouns name things.

Likewise, through using his whole body to act out the written cues that tell him to do something, he is learning that there is a group of words that involve action. This will make for an ah-ha! moment when you—or his future teacher—explain that these are called verbs.

Now you can begin to draw his attention to words that describe things:

"How many words can we think of to tell us more about this bunny?" (gray, little, soft, quiet, fluffy, squirmy . . .)

ADJECTIVES: WORDS THAT DESCRIBE

Size	Color	Shape	Properties	Texture	Feelings	Characteristics
big	red	round	heavy	smooth	sad	quiet
small	blue	square	light	rough	happy	wiggly
huge	green	triangular	solid	bumpy	mad	fast
teeny	yellow	rectangular	bouncy	slippery	worried	slow
large	pink	pointed	cold	prickly	excited	noisy

By now you get the picture: our language is loaded with adjectives. Use them with your sweet, little, excited, wiggly, teachable, loveable, indispensable ones!

Show him how some words show relationship:

> "Here is a little black stone. Can you put it *on* the table? . . . *under* the table? . . . *beside* the table?"

PREPOSITIONS: WORDS THAT SHOW RELATIONSHIP

above	before	between	inside	over
against	behind	by	near	under
around	below	from	off	with
at	beside	in	on	without

This is a partial list—appropriate for five to seven year olds.

Here you are laying the groundwork for future language studies, giving your child experience with how words work in our language. He will benefit from this later when he learns the parts of speech: nouns, verbs, adjectives, and prepositions.

Make sure your child understands the way we use comparative and superlative:

"Which shirt is larger—this one or that one?"

"Which of these three balls is the biggest? The smallest?"

Again, we don't introduce the terminology now; just practice with the language.

Now's the time to start asking him about

- rhyming words

- synonyms (words that mean the same)

- antonyms (words that mean the opposite)

- homonyms (words that sound the same but have different spellings and meanings

At this point you don't use those terms. Just gently draw his attention to the way our language works by asking:

"Can you think of a word that rhymes with *tell*?"

"Is there a word that means the same thing as *big*?"

"What is the opposite of *hot*?"

"The wind *blew* a *blue* kite. Are there two words that sound the same?"

You will find lists of these word pairs at 🍎 .

Working with Letters

Siblings make great teachers!

Continue to work on writing skills. Begin by teaching your child proper writing posture. Make sure your child has a child-friendly place to write, something that takes his smaller size into consideration. He needs a stable, smooth writing surface. He needs to have his feet resting firmly on something solid. Show him how to tilt the paper so that the bottom left corner is pointing at his belly button. Show him how to use his left hand to hold the paper in position (see appendix I for lefties). Show him how to lean forward slightly and how to move his writing arm across the paper.

Begin with the letters that are easiest to form (*l, o, i, c*). Write one per line on lined paper (preferably the elementary ruled wide sheets). Let your child trace around the letter you have written, then continue making them on his own ("Let's try to make each one a little more beautiful than the last"). To help a child with weaker motor skills, fill the line yourself with letters of dotted lines (templates for dotted letters and all writing exercises at 🍎. Then he can trace around the dots.

Once your child has practiced a number of letters, he can begin to write phonetic words instead of using the magnetic letters. Show him how to leave a space between words on a line.

Since your child will not need uppercase letters until he is writing sentences, you can wait until that time to have him practice writing them. By then he will have come across them one at a time in his own reading, so they will be familiar.

When teaching a child to write letters, use lowercase also.

Your child may have already picked up from Sesame Street or elsewhere that besides sounds, letters also have names. Some children have no difficulty with memorizing both simultaneously; but for others it's a stretch. For the latter especially it's important not to burden them with memorizing names until after reading is established. Then you can teach the names of letters, explaining, "You know this letter makes the sound *rrr*. The name of the letter is *R*."

If your child has not already picked it up elsewhere, now's the time to teach the alphabet in sequence. If it seems late, because every three-year-old on your street knows the alphabet song, think about it: the only reason we need to know the alphabet in sequence is to look things up in the dictionary—a skill the child isn't introduced to until at least a year after he reads.

Expanding Vocabulary

Through reading and conversation, try to give your child the richest vocabulary you can. At this point you should be talking to your child—at least in terms of the words you choose—the same way you would talk to an adult.

A broad vocabulary not only expands the child's mastery of his environment, it also expands his ability to perceive. When we go by a construction site and comment on the commotion, the powerful equipment, the workers' skill, the effect on the surrounding buildings, we stir our children's imagination and attention to detail. It's like opening windows in their minds.

Try to reach beyond *nice, good, bad, OK,* for words that more accurately describe how things are. Offer verbal fill-in-the-blanks:

"Red is a color that looks so_____"

"When my dog sees me, he acts _____"

When your child is caught up in an emotion, give him the name for it:

"Are you feeling jealous?"

Now it's time to start attaching abstract words like *courage, faith,* and *loyalty* to those stories you're reading. Just remember, they will only have meaning if they are linked to something specific in the child's mind.

Stimulating Creativity

If we want our children to have a healthy curiosity about life and living—which is what will make them better readers and better learners—we need to encourage this in the early years.

Talk with your child about everything. Look at him while he talks. Through your questions, encourage him to make the most of his observation, thinking, and reasoning skills. Ask open-ended questions:

Not: "Did you have a good time at the park?"

But: "What did you enjoy about the park today?"

When your child draws a picture, ask him to tell you about it and let him watch you as you write his words on the picture. Show him this is like making a book. In fact, he can draw many pictures and you can staple them together to make his own book. You can write the story on the pages as he tells it to you.

Another fun project you can do with your child is to start a diary with him—before he can write it himself. Explain to him what a diary is all about, how it helps us to remember important things we've done or people we've met or feelings we've had. Then open the diary with him each day and ask him what he would like you to write down for him.

Providing Enrichment

Provide your child with as much exposure as possible to art and music—not just his own hands-on efforts, but encounters with the classics.

Small art reproductions (easy to find in greeting card form) hung at his eye level offer opportunities for many open-ended questions, encouraging your child to think and use his imagination. Boys especially love Winslow Homer's work: the boys playing crack-the-whip and the fishermen racing home before the storm are rich in conversation possibilities.

I didn't grow up with much exposure to classical music myself, but I have enjoyed learning more as an adult. Playing some Mozart or Haydn can have an incomparable calming effect on the day that's gotten a little too rowdy. And did you know studies show just listening to classical music boosts IQ levels?

My children and I get up half an hour earlier than we have to just to sing some hymns together before we start our day. The poetry is so beautiful—I often draw inspiration from a line of a hymn and give an on-the-spot spiritual lesson. As I once heard author and lecturer Florence Littauer say, "Where two or more children are gathered, Mom will give a sermon."

Read poetry and memorize it with your children. Sing lots of songs—all types of songs with them. Don't worry about your voice. They are sure to think it's the most beautiful voice in the world; where else will you find such an appreciative audience? Try to sing every day.

Don't do it because you should; do it because it's fun!

Developing Humor

Since your baby's first laugh, hasn't his sense of humor been special to you? Don't his giggles and guffaws still make your heart merry? Keep them coming and motivate your early reader to read a little extra with joke and riddle books from the library. Each of my children in their earliest reading days enjoyed reading riddles to me.

"Why did the chicken cross the road?"

"To get to the other side." (Hey, this is easy.)

"Why did the gumball cross the road?"

"Why?" (Obviously someone's been doing some thinking to keep us parents on our toes!)

"Because it was stuck to the chicken's foot!"

Humorous poetry and tongue twisters are sure to grab his attention as well.

As your child matures, he will begin to appreciate more subtle humor, especially with you beside him to smile at the appropriate moments. For instance, I've always found the description of the little duck's family in *The Story about Ping* to be hilarious—maybe because of our big family. Simply through your voice inflection, you can highlight the humor in the books you read with your child.

Ordering Reality

It is largely through language that we are able to perceive the order in the universe. A child of four or five is beginning to understand that life is not random. This is the appropriate time to give him all the language he needs to understand weather, seasons, days of the week, months of the year, times of day.

Give him a beginning sense of classification skills with the following fun game: sort toys into various groups:

- stuffed toys

- building toys

- toys made of wood/plastic/metal

- toys with wheels/immovable toys

- toys you play with indoors/outdoors

- toys you play with by yourself/with friends

- large toys/small toys

- toys that need batteries/toys that don't

- toys with one part/toys with many

Stretch your child in his ability to think sequentially. Begin with one or two directions, either fun or useful:

"Skip to the end of our sidewalk and twirl three times."

"Please take this bowl to the kitchen and bring me a dishtowel."

Then, as your child shows he can successfully carry out the directions, begin adding more at a time:

"Shut your eyes, then wiggle your nose, then turn around, and sit down."

"Please get out your lunchbox, put in a container of yogurt from the fridge, a banana, a spoon, and a napkin."

Building your child's skills in classification and following directions gives him a feeling of security—understanding and participating in the order around him.

Perfecting Grammar

By the time a child is four or five, he has mastered the basic structure of his language. The grammar mistakes your child might be making at this point are more subtle than the obvious ones he was making as a toddler—often errors a significant number of adults make as well (if your own grammar could use a brush-up, all you need is a good, traditional fifth-grade language workbook). At this age, you will want him to be conscious of the correction, but you can do it in the most positive way by a technique called "mirroring":

"Her and I want to go to the store."

"Her and I?"

"She and I . . ."

✳ ✳ ✳

"Our team didn't do so good today."

"Didn't do so good or didn't do so well?"

"Didn't do so well."

Reinforcing Basics

"What do you think about workbooks?" is a question I hear frequently. My answer? I love workbooks.

I think workbooks have gotten a bad rap in recent years because of the de-emphasis on structure in public schools. I've met a lot of teachers who have few kind words for workbooks. Yet the truth is, I have never met a child who didn't like them.

I said earlier that a child will pick up all the rules, exceptions, and outrageous things about our language just through reading. Still, it never hurts to make sure he's seen it all. And for a slower learner, a phonics workbook will break reading components into bite-size pieces, boosting the child's confidence as he makes a little progress each day.

A good phonics workbook is an invaluable asset in sharpening your child's language skills. I have my own favorites, which I share in appendix J.

Giving Encouragement

The greatest asset your child has in his early reading days is you. Your praise and encouragement will give your child confidence and a sense of security as he tries his wings. He needs to know you have faith in his abilities. As long as he has confidence, he will be eager to keep reading.

Never label a child or make him feel inadequate. An encouraging word goes a long way: "I know this might seem hard to you now; it does to a lot of kids who learn to read. Don't worry. In a few days you'll know it so well you'll never remember that you thought it was hard."

Some children do need more time and practice than others. If you have a slower learner, rather than feeling frustrated or self-critical, be grateful that you are teaching him yourself. These are the children who especially need to be taught at home. At school, without the one-on-one attention, they'd just slip through the cracks.

TEACHING TIPS

What works	What doesn't work
Patience	Impatience
Confidence	Too high expectations
Flexibility	Distractions
Ability to assess child's	Lack of sensitivity to
strengths and weaknesses	child's limits

Remember: Prayer does wonders for the child you teach and for you as well!

Getting the Whole Picture

So much of reading is not just deciphering words on the page, but what we bring to the experience ourselves. Part of enabling your child to become the best reader he can be is building up his language skills in every way you can.

So the areas I've mentioned so far—recognizing words, building vocabulary, perfecting grammar, reinforcing basics—are all part of the package your child brings to the experience of reading. The stronger he is in these areas, the more capable a reader he will be; the more capable a reader he is, the more he will enjoy reading; the more he enjoys reading, the stronger he will be in all these areas—grammar, vocabulary, and . . . well, by now you get the picture, I'm sure.

Anything we can do to build our children's language or reading skills will spill over into all the areas. So even if you only have time to do a little, do a little. In the area of language, as in all of parenting, a little means a lot.

Introducing Readers

Now comes the fun part—introducing readers. I remember when I first started teaching twenty-some years ago. This was the hardest area for us as teachers. We'd get our kids all ready for phonetic reading and then there just weren't any interesting phonetic readers available.

No such problem now. There are some wonderful sets of early readers—enjoyable stories by good writers—available at discount stores like Wal-Mart or online at Amazon or at your library. (See the end of this chapter for lists.)

I start out with *Bob Books* (see Book Recommendations at the end of this chapter), which are almost completely phonetic and begin with only a few words and a cute drawing on each page. This gets the child used to the idea that sentences

- are composed of words and spaces,

- begin with capital letters,

- end with periods, and

- often contain sight words like *a* and *the.*

At the same time, they boost any child's confidence by making it possible for him to read a whole book by himself. What a wonderful job these authors have done!

In addition to having plenty of books available, what your child will need now is your undivided attention. At this point in his reading journey, you need to put in time listening to him and guiding his progress as he reads aloud. At the very beginning, you may want to hold the book and point to the words as he reads them. Some children need a little extra time getting the hang of the flow of words on the page. This helps build their reading left-to-right, one-line-after-another skill.

As he reads, your child will encounter all the exceptions and strangely constructed words that we have postponed while taking the phonetic approach. However, because of his success with phonetic reading, your child will tackle these words with confidence. And because you are there to guide his beginning reading, he will develop *word-attack skills* through

- the systematic or casual introduction of nonphonetic combinations,

- a growing sight vocabulary (words not decipherable any other way), and

- figuring out words in context.

Now the secret about reading is this: getting a child ready is where most of the work goes on. And each stage can take different amounts of time for different children. Some children take a long time of playing the Sound Game before they "get it"—that words are made up of individual sounds. Some children take a long time making the connection between the sound and the symbol. But even if a child has spent a lot of time at any particular pre-reading stage, don't assume that his explosion into reading will be slow.

In the beginning of the book, I shared my experience with my daughter Sophia, whose developmental timetable was more than a year behind what I had come to expect through all my work with children. Though she didn't read until she was seven, within six months she was reading at second-grade level.

There was also my son Zachary, who seemed to take forever to pick up ten letters so that we could start phonetic combinations. Yet once he did, at age five and a half, within a year he was reading at third-grade level. By eight he was reading at a tenth-grade level. Don't limit your child's progress by labeling him as slow just because he took a little longer in one area than you might have expected.

I insert this caveat here because sometimes the shift from reading one word at a time to reading sentences fluently can take a little time. You may have to sit through many readings of *Bob Books* before you see the results you want. If this is the case, be patient. Keep building up your child in all the other areas of language skills discussed above. Keep reading books to him. And keep encouraging him.

At some point—provided your child has not become discouraged and given up—as though you had reached the top of the roller coaster, your child will begin zooming down a track of his own. Reading will become easy and fun.

Now a world of wonderful early readers is waiting for him (see Book Recommendations on page 125). And he will also begin reading some of the books that have become best friends through all the hours you've spent reading. Books like *The Cat in the Hat*, *Green Eggs and Ham*, and *Go, Dog, Go* are perfect confidence builders. Because the child knows them well, he will be able to figure out many sight words and make them his own.

Be careful not to give your child books above his reading level. It's a good idea to keep stretching him vocabulary-wise, but in the early reading days more than a few unfamiliar words per page are too many.

Soon he will be reading completely independently. Encourage him to read as much as possible. If he is a reluctant reader, structure a one-hour reading time into your day when you read your own book while he reads his.

Once a child is reading independently, many things fall into place. Given plenty of reading material and time to read, a child can actually develop an impressive vocabulary, perfect grammar, and excellent spelling—with minimal intervention from you.

This is the secret of why homeschooling works to produce great students with significantly higher test scores: so much of learning is reading based. Once a child is a fluent reader, he can teach himself anything. The world becomes an open book.

Building Comprehension

Make the most of your child's experience with early readers by building his reading comprehension. Instead of closing the book and putting it away when you're finished, ask questions:

- about the main idea,

- the order and sequence of events,

- the characters,

- the setting, and

- the important details.

Ask him to summarize:

"What happened in the story?"

Encourage him to make judgments:

"Did you think the boy did the right thing?"

"What would you have done?"

"Why did you like the story?"

Reading Aloud

Just because your child is reading solo, don't stop reading aloud. And though you are careful to make sure that the books he reads himself are at his reading level, your own reading to your child can be well above; in fact, they can be at yours.

For twenty years my husband, Tripp, has read nightly to our children, including many classics (*Treasure Island, David Copperfield*) and works as sophisticated as *The Lord of the Rings* trilogy. In listening to stories, your child does not have to understand every word. He will absorb the richness of the language and a lot of meaning simply through context and the drama with which you read.

In addition, this early experience of listening to a grown-up read grown-up literature establishes a pattern of how the child will read when he reads to himself. If he has first heard the classics read with enthusiasm and emotion, he will bring these qualities to his own reading later on.

His comprehension will be better also. A child who has spent a lot of time concentrating and listening will find it easy to read without distraction from within or without. He'll be able to follow the author's thoughts page after page.

Perhaps most of all, he will bring to his reading experience all the warmth and good feeling that is his through the special moments he has shared with the people most important to him in all the world—his parents.

Tripp's nightly reading has not only built a special bond between him and the children, but also between our children and good literature. Our family life has been greatly enriched by the cozy hours he has spent.

Think of this: in twenty years no one will remember whether you finished cleaning up before you went to bed each night. Neither will they remember if you solved that programming problem or landed that important customer. But your children will always remember the books you read, the talks you had, and the lessons they learned at your knee.

Both Tripp and I can say with assurance that you will look back on the times you have spent reading to your children as some of the best-spent hours of your life.

Reading Tips

Books for this age are so exciting! What a wonder that simply by turning the pages of a book we can give our children an up close and personal look at life on the other side of the globe, or the other side of the century! Or serve up a tale meant to help them cope with their problems or build their character. Or share with them our history or our faith.

Your five-to-seven-year-old is now ready to be introduced to an abundance of life—the broadest spectrum of races, places, cultures, and historical periods. He needs to know that even in our own country—even in our own hometown—not everyone lives the same way. Especially if your child lives in comfortable circumstances, he needs to know that others live in need.

But he also needs to know that material circumstances don't say much at all about the things that truly make life worth living. As in *A Chair for My Mother,* a family can go through many ups and downs and yet find great joy in something small and simple.

Values-building starts earlier than we might think. At five years old, children are really beginning to size up the world and the adults around them. They have a lot of questions regarding right and wrong. They want answers.

At this age, the most appropriate way to teach values is through stories. In *The Little Red Lighthouse and the Great Gray Bridge,* children see arrogance projected onto a protagonist who isn't even human. This makes it safe to look at. Remember, Jesus taught grown-ups by parables about real situations, not by abstract talks about virtues. We can do the same with our children.

When possible, preview a book before reading it with your child so you can make sure you understand the message. Take it from a writer: every writer has an agenda. When we read a book to our children, we need to know that the agenda behind it is compatible with our own. Of course, this means you need to be very clear about your own.

Whatever you do, don't leave your children empty to absorb the values of popular culture, of television and movies. Take a proactive approach. Have a plan. Decide what's important to your family and then back it up by making sure the books you give your child, as much as the shows you let him watch, are compatible with your values.

If in doubt, skip it. There's too much good stuff out there to waste time on books that undermine the values you hold dear. And there's so much that will stretch you and your children in a positive direction.

Book Recommendations
Five to Seven Years

Read-Aloud Stories

(Once again, though there are newer editions of these books available, I have used the original year of publication to provide some idea of the timelessness and staying-power of children's books that have become classics.)

Alexander and the Terrible, Horrible, No Good, Very Bad Day, Judith Viorst, Aladdin, 1972.

Everyone has a really bad day now and then. Alexander gives us a language for sharing it and accepting it. Contemporary and funny.

Blueberries for Sal, Robert McCloskey, Puffin Books, 1948.

What happens when a little girl and a little bear wander away from their blueberry-picking mothers and switch who they follow? A beautifully illustrated story sets a lovely mood, then introduces just enough suspense for children.

A Chair for My Mother, Vera B. Williams, Mulberry, 1982.

A remarkably beautiful story told by a young girl whose mother is a waitress. Since they lost all their furniture in a fire, they've been saving mother's tips in a jar so they can buy a big comfortable chair for their whole family to enjoy—daughter, mother, and grandmother. Life has its ups and downs, but there's always lots of love.

Frog and Toad Are Friends (and other *Frog and Toad* books), Arnold Lobel, Harpercollins, 1970.

A pair of loveable best friends spend the summer watching out for and bringing out the best in each other. Doubles as an early reader.

George Shrinks, William Joyce, Scholastic, 1985.

Nothing heavy, just a romp for the imagination when George dreams he is small and wakes up the size of a peanut. Your child will love the pictures, in which George flies for the mail in a toy airplane.

Goops and How to Be Them: A Manual of Manners for Polite Infants Inculcating Many Juvenile Virtues Both by Precept and Example, With 90 Drawings (also *More Goops*), Gelett Burgess, Dover Publications, republished 1968.

"The Goops they lick their fingers, and the Goops they lick their knives; they spill their broth on tablecloth—Oh, they lead disgusting lives!" This old-fashioned compendium of poems on manners is just plain hilarious—and one of the easiest ways to teach children manners.

Harold and the Purple Crayon, Crockett Johnson, Harpercollins, 1955.

An ingenious tale: Harold goes out for a walk with a purple crayon in his hand—and draws himself all kinds of adventures, showing some common sense and good problem-solving skills along the way.

The Hole in the Dike, retold by Norma Green, Scholastic, 1974.

As the author states at the end of the book, this tale was spun a hundred years ago by a woman who had never been to Holland. And yet it so symbolized the struggle of the Dutch that they erected a statue to the boy who saved his country from floods. A tale that underscores sacrifice and loyalty to one's country.

Least of All, Carol Purdy, Aladdin, 1987.

The youngest of six children—and the only girl—Raven Hannah is not big enough to help with any of the work on her family's farm. But when she teaches herself to read from the Bible, she finds that as the first reader in the family, she has a unique gift to offer.

The Lion and the Mouse, A. J. Wood, illustrated by Ian Andrew, Millbrook Press, 1995.

Aesop's classic fable, beloved by readers throughout the ages, of a mighty lion who spares the life of a mouse and is amply repaid for his mercy.

The Little House, Virginia Lee Burton, Scholastic, 1942.

"Once upon a time there was a little house way out in the country. She was a pretty Little House and she was strong and well built." The contrast between the Little House's peaceful existence with the beautiful seasons and her life when a big city grows around her makes for a touching tale. The deeper theme: progress has a price. Children will love the pictures, the happy ending, and the lesson learned by the Little House.

Little People in Tough Spots: Bible Answers for Young Children, V. Gilbert Beers, Thomas Nelson, 1992.

This gem of a book shows children in an easy-to-understand way that the answers to life's problems are in the Bible. Pick a problem—"I'm scared," "I have too much to do," "Do I have to share?"—and you will find a vignette of a child here and now who faces the problem, then draws inspiration from a particular person in the Bible.

The Little Red Lighthouse and the Great Gray Bridge, Hildegarde H. Swift, Harcourt Brace, 1942.

A little lighthouse on the Hudson River starts out with a little too much pride, suffers great humiliation when the George Washington Bridge is built, and finally gains a properly modest confidence when it finds that it is useful and has an important job to do.

Ox-Cart Man, Donald Hall, Viking Press, 1979.

This lyrical journey through the seasons with a serene and productive nineteenth-century rural New England family will give your child (and you) a feeling for our country's heritage.

People, Peter Spier, Doubleday, 1980.

An incredibly rich, child-friendly resource of information about the diversity of people and cultures. Beautiful and absorbing illustrations, beginning with Adam and Eve in the Garden of Eden, then covering all sorts of human complexities since. This is a book your child will spend hours with and learn much from.

Pretzel, Margaret Rey, Scholastic, 1944.

My thirty-year-old daughter Jasmine's favorite love story—the tale of a prize-winning dachshund who can't win the heart of the dog across the street. Unimpressed by the physical qualities that others admire, she finally finds something to admire about herself. Marriage and family are the ultimate prize in this old-fashioned heartwarming story.

Read-N-Grow Picture Bible, Word Books, 1979.

Two thousand pictures (six per page, with a sentence or two under each) will take your child through the Bible from start to finish. My children have loved this motivational format, which has really reinforced the historical continuity of the Bible.

St. Jerome and the Lion, Margaret Hodges, Orchard Books, 1991.

Jerome, the medieval monk who lived in Bethlehem and translated the Bible into Latin, earns the devotion of a lion by removing a thorn from his paw. When the monastery's donkey is stolen, the other monks accuse the lion of having eaten it, but only Jerome refuses to condemn him and is proven right.

The Story About Ping, Marjorie Flack, Viking Press, 1933.

A lilting and funny story about a little duck who lives with his comically large family on a boat on the Yangtze River in China. One day while searching for food, he finds himself left behind. Bravely, he goes in search of his family, finding many adventures along the way.

The Story of Babar, Jean De Brunhoff, Random House, 1931.

This book—originally written in French—has delighted children and adults for decades. The story of an elephant who loses his mother to hunters, wanders to the city, buys a new wardrobe, becomes the hit of society, marries Celeste, and is crowned King of the Elephants.

The Story of Ferdinand, Munro Leaf, Scholastic, 1936.

One of the best-selling children's books of all time, about a peaceful bull who would rather sit beneath a tree smelling flowers than fight in the bull ring.

William Tell, Margaret Early, Harry N. Abrams, 1991.

A story of courage and purpose: the fourteenth-century Swiss folk hero is forced to shoot an apple from his son's head by the evil governor, then leads his countrymen into action against Austria's tyranny. He remains a man who thinks of himself more as a husband and father than a hero.

The Year at Maple Hill Farm, Alice & Martin Provensen, Aladdin, 1978.

A year in the country with all its seasonal changes—the work, play, and rewards of life on a farm.

°°° Check 🍎 for expanded list.°°°

Early Readers

Bob Books for Beginning Readers (sets 1–5), Bobby Lynn Maslen, Scholastic Publications 2006 (available at www.bobbooks.com, www.amazon.com, or www.walmart.com).

When they first appeared in the early eighties, these wonderful first phonetic readers were the answer to many teachers' prayers. Written by a mother of four and illustrated by her husband, they have now sold more than two million copies.

Bob Books will give your child a bridge from reading single words to reading real books. Reading these will reinforce his phonetic skills, introduce capital letters, periods, and important sight words—but most importantly will build his confidence: "Hey, I'm reading a book!"

Step into Reading Books, various titles and authors, Random House.

More than one hundred fun and friendly early readers, divided into four reading levels.

I Can Read Books, various titles and authors, Harper Trophy.

A little more complex (and longer) than the books in the *Step into Reading* series, these are a good follow-up.

Both the *Step into Reading* books and the *I Can Read* books are sold at Wal-Mart and Target as well as Borders. Or find them at www.walmart.com or www.amazon.com by searching for *Step into Reading* or *I Can Read*. At Amazon, if your order totals more than twenty-five dollars, be sure to request free shipping. Also, look for bargains on eBay or check your local library.

A Beka Books, First Grade Reader series.

I have used these—as well as the ones that follow for higher grades—with all my children. They are old-fashioned and wholesome. The stories do more than flex the child's reading muscles, they help build character. Each story is followed by comprehension questions, which will train your child to listen to what he is reading, thus helping him become a better learner.

You can find them on eBay or at www.abeka.com.

CHAPTER 4

Language-Based Studies:
History and Song

History

A LITTLE CHILD DOES NOT NEED to study history as a series of events. That kind of learning will come later. Remember, the young child is not capable of abstract thinking. He only has a few years experience and little understanding of time at all, much less periods of time long before he was born.

And really that is how the child—who naturally views himself as the center of the universe—begins to grasp the concept of time. There was the time before he was born and the time since. Anytime you sit down with a photo album, on line or on your lap, you are teaching him history—his own story.

The child matures and begins to be interested in things outside himself. There are photos of family events that occurred before he was born. People talk about things that happened before, things that will happen in the future. The child begins to have a sense of time as a continuum.

As we draw his attention to the seasons, as we teach him how we tell hours by the clock and days by the calendar, we are helping him develop a sense of past, present, and future. But this is very rudimentary. Someday—when he is eight or so—he will be introduced to time lines and visible representations of longer periods of time. Then he will begin to understand.

In the meantime, though we can't teach the subject in a linear fashion, there is much we can do to lay a foundation for the child's later study of history. In the same manner in which we begin to familiarize our children with the Bible through stories extracted from our spiritual history, we can begin to introduce our cultural heritage through stories—true stories—of men and women whose actions shaped history and whose character exemplified attributes we want to encourage in our children.

In the best of all teaching worlds, history and character development go hand in hand. Keep in mind that you are not just instilling your child with facts, but preparing him to take his place in history. Children love stories of noble men and women, especially those that begin with chapters from their childhoods. You may read these stories aloud, or once your children are reading, they will enjoy reading them themselves. You may also listen to them on tape or watch videos. (See list of resources that follows.)

The following are some historical figures your child will eventually need to know. You can begin around age five to introduce bits and pieces of their personal history:

Abigail Adams	Thomas Edison
Johnny Appleseed	George F. Handel
Clara Barton	Mahalia Jackson
Robert Boyle	Stonewall Jackson
William Bradford	Thomas Jefferson
William Jennings Bryan	Helen Keller
George Washington Carver	Johannes Kepler
Christopher Columbus	Francis Scott Key
Stephen Douglas	Robert E. Lee

Lewis & Clark	Paul Revere
Abraham Lincoln	Billy Sunday
David Livingstone	Teresa of Calcutta
Samuel F. Morse	Harriet Tubman
Isaac Newton	George Washington
Florence Nightingale	Noah Webster
Louis Pasteur	Susannah Wesley
Pocahantas	The Wright Brothers

Here is a list of resources:

The Sower Series, Mott Media—Twenty-seven inspirational biographies of Christians who've changed the course of history—including political leaders, inventors, soldiers, scientists. Reading level states nine to fourteen, but parents can read them to kids much earlier, and early readers may be ready for them at seven. (www.mottmedia.com/sower.html)

Step into Reading Series, Random House—Among this set of early readers (billed as grades one to three, but you can read them to your child sooner) are stories of Christopher Columbus, George Washington, Ben Franklin, Paul Revere, Lewis and Clark, Harriet Tubman, to name a few. It also includes a few significant events such as the first Thanksgiving, the first landing on the moon, and the acquisition of the Statue of Liberty.

Nest Entertainment Animated Heroes Classics—A collection of twenty DVDs, each with a story of an important historical figure. (www.nestfamily.com)

Biographies for Children: Famous Leaders for Young Readers—This generous online resource offers thirty-seven biographies, including pictures, worksheets, music, and games—all absolutely free and attractively formatted. (www.garde nofpraise.com/leaders.htm)

Song

Let your days with your child be filled with song. I can promise you that you will always be glad you did. The gift of singing is something any parent can give; it is absolutely free and absolutely priceless.

As a child who wasn't encouraged to sing and didn't have many opportunities, I was very self-conscious about my voice. As an adult, I would never have dreamed of singing in front of anyone.

As a teacher, though, I had to lead twenty-five children under six each day in song. Singing each day—even children's songs—improved my voice immensely, as did the look of adoration in the children's eyes when I would introduce a new song. I discovered firsthand the power of song to bond children's hearts to their teachers. Music plays a big part in why children love preschool.

As I asked in *Mommy, Teach Me!*: Why send your child to preschool to fall in love with his teacher? Why not create the same rich learning environment at home—one that meets his developmental needs—to go on building the bonds that will eventually keep him true to the core values you teach no matter where his educational path takes him?

After becoming Christians and beginning our homeschool journey, we joined early in the morning for devotions, which included at least twenty minutes of sing-ing—hymns for the older members of the family who could read and comprehend the rich theology within the verses, and more simple praise choruses that even the youngest children could join in.

Song is so important! Certainly David understood that, as he learned to speak to his heavenly Father in song—whether it was rejoicing or crying out for help. Song adds richness and intimacy as well as courage to express feelings we might not otherwise be able to express. To bring up a child who feels comfortable with song should be the goal of every parent.

In the same way hymns and praise choruses give depth and meaning to our individual and collective spiritual experience, traditional folk songs serve to ground and focus children, as well as to enrich the connections they need to make with their surroundings and their culture.

I didn't understand this at first. But because I wanted to create the richest learning experience for my children at home, I also devoted a time every day to singing the songs I'd sung with kids in preschool: from "The Itsy-Bitsy Spider" and "The Wheels on the Bus"—which reinforce language, imagination, and participation—to more sophisticated songs like "She'll Be Comin' 'Round the Mountain" and "Polly Wolly Doodle."

What I mean by more sophisticated—and what I've come to see in retrospect about the importance of this kind of singing at home—is this: there is a lexicon of songs from our nation's history that are part of our shared cultural experience. Through singing a song like "I've Been Workin' on the Railroad," the child does more than learn about a historical event; he participates in it, while at the same time providing some framework for his future study of the Transcontinental Railroad. Certainly the feeling captured by the song—the unquenchable American workaday spirit of the nineteenth century—is every bit as important as memorizing the date the final spike was driven.

As one music professional explains: "Music has always been what anthropologists call a 'culture carrier' . . . if you perform it, you own a little bit of American culture in a way that's far more profound."[8]

These American classics are actually disappearing from our collective awareness, as documented by Marilyn Ward, PhD, who surveyed four thousand elementary and high-school music teachers—eighty from each state—to determine their students' familiarity. The disappointing news: kids generally knew only 20 percent of the list of one hundred classic songs.[9]

Today, we are blessed with some singers who create children's music that is fun and entertaining (and more intelligent than the Wiggles) for children and adults, and whom I don't hesitate to recommend. But as parents, we need to be aware of the big picture: what are our goals for our children and what do we need to get them there? Some of the simplest, sweetest children's songs come packed with a lesson: "If You're Happy and You Know It" is all about attitude; "Five Little Ducks" is all about security; and "Over in the Meadow" (tune and lyrics at 🍎) is a ten-part lesson in obedience.

Trend wise, the emphasis in today's children's music seems to be on self—understanding emotions, dealing with everyday problems, learning to be friends. These lessons all have their place, but not to the exclusion of the child's learning of events that are bigger and more significant than himself. No one needs a constant diet of anything that reinforces our mistaken and immature notion that the world revolves around us.

Music can be an experience that lifts your child out of himself and into a larger place and time. And you can have fun while you explore this realm with him. The long-term benefits of raising children who love to lift their voices in song is that they will continue to do so even when they are grown, filling your home with harmony. I do not play an instrument and never had a voice lesson, but I think part of the reason three of my twelve are pursuing careers in music is because those doors were opened wide in the years that make the most difference—the early ones.

The following are a few lists of classic songs as well as recommended children's singers. Check 🍎 for more recommendations, lyrics, and melodies.

Twenty-Five Toddler Classics

"Old McDonald"

"B-I-N-G-O"

"Roll Over"

"Farmer in the Dell"

"Five Little Ducks"

"Head and Shoulders"

"Hokey Pokey"

"Twinkle, Twinkle Little Star"

"Wheels on the Bus"

"Itsy Bitsy Spider"

"This Old Man"

"If You're Happy and You Know It"

"Row, Row, Row Your Boat"

"Hickory, Dickory, Dock"

"Here We Go 'Round the Mulberry Bush"

"Deep and Wide"

"London Bridge"

"Jack and Jill"

"The Muffin Man"

"Pop Goes the Weasel"

"Do Your Ears Hang Low"

"The More We Get Together"

"Jesus Loves Me"

"Jesus Loves the Little Children"

"Over in the Meadow"

Twenty-Five American Classics

"Yankee Doodle"

"This Little Light of Mine"

"I've Been Workin' on the Railroad"

"She'll Be Comin' 'Round the Mountain"

"This Land Is Your Land"

"Amazing Grace"

"America, the Beautiful"

"Home on the Range"

"Polly Wolly Doodle"

"You Are My Sunshine"

"Bicycle Built for Two"

"Down in the Valley"

"Skip to My Lou"

"Shenandoah"

"My Darling Clementine"

"Old Kentucky Home"

"Michael, Row the Boat Ashore"

"When Johnny Comes Marching Home Again"

"Turkey in the Straw"

"The Erie Canal"

"Dixie"

"Joshua Fit the Battle of Jericho"

"Battle Hymn of the Republic"

"Shoo Fly"

"Oh, Susannah"

A few modern songsters who are lots of fun
Raffi
Joe Scruggs
Hap Palmer

Don't forget—look for more recommendations at 🍎 —and share some of your own!

CHAPTER
5

HAPPY ENDINGS

THE ROOM I WORK IN HOLDS my desk and computer and files and reference books—all the things it takes for me to write. But it's so much more than an office, as the walls are lined with bookshelves and there are usually children here. As I write, they wander in and out looking for books, then settle on the loveseat for a good read. Their dad and I somehow passed on our love of books, and they are like friends, a presence in every room of the house, something that unites and enriches our family as we talk and share about them.

It started small, with our first purchase of books for our children and the practice of reading nightly. We read the best-loved stories over and over again. Some of the kids' books on our shelves are thirty years old and have entertained all twelve of our children.

When it came time to share my recommendations in this book, I simply went through our shelves and pulled the books I *knew* were the most loved and read. Like *Corduroy*, the stuffed bear who's lost his shiny new appearance because he's been so loveable, these books showed the telltale signs of their popularity.

Now, once again, I'm sitting in the midst of a tempting array of our very favorite books, and thinking that because once again I've been so busy writing, it's been a while since I've read most of them. Also I've discovered some of the ones I read a gazillion times to my older children somehow have been overlooked with the younger ones. I've realized I now have a whole new generation of children to enjoy these books with again.

And so I'm pretty excited. Excited not only to share through this book and interactive 🍎 the reading approach that's worked so well for our family, but excited because I've been reminded of some wonderful books that I'll now have a lot more time to read!

Keep up the good work you've started on the road to reading. You'll discover that teaching your children to read is not just another happy ending. It's really a great beginning!

APPENDIX
A

Magazines

MAGAZINES CAN STIMULATE A LOT OF reading in children who might be reluctant to tackle a whole book. (Sound like any adults you know?) Think of magazines as a *positive* resource to get your child hooked on reading, to open vistas to other cultures, classes, and concerns. Encourage your child to share—perhaps at the dinner table—what he has learned from the articles he has read.

Here is the best in children's magazines:

Focus on the Family Clubhouse (Ages 8–12) and *Clubhouse Jr.* (Ages 4–8)

Monthly 24-page magazine, filled with articles and stories relevant to kids' lives. Yearly subscription $18. (www.family.org or call 800-232-6459)

God's World

Weekly newspaper published in five editions—kindergarten through junior high—featuring current events from a Christian perspective. Yearly subscription $21.95, available at www.gwnews.com (where you can also download a free sample) and 800-951-5437. Discount for groups.

Highlights For Kids (Ages 2–12)

Monthly 42-page magazine, chock-full of stories, games, and puzzles to get your child used to thinking logically. Yes, it's the same one you read when you were a child, and still appeals! One-year subscription $29.64; three-year $60.12. Order at www.highlights.com or call 800-255-9517.

Kids Discover (Ages 6–12, but older kids and parents will enjoy it too!)

Ten issues a year, each devoted to a specific topic, such as Ancient China, Royalty, Washington, DC. Beautifully illustrated and full of interesting facts. One-year subscription $19.95. Visit www.kidsdiscover.com or call 800-825-2821.

Sports Illustrated for Kids (Ages 8 and up)

Monthly magazine guaranteed to get even the balkiest boy reading—as long as he loves sports! One-year subscription $24.95. Visit www.sikids.com or call 800-826-0083.

Be good stewards with magazines: pass them on to school libraries or hospitals with pediatric units.

Comfort

WHEN I'M FEELING DOWN AND DISCOURAGED, like I'm just never going to get this parenting thing down perfectly (much less teach anyone to read), I find comfort in these verses:

> *But those who hope in the LORD*
> *will renew their strength.*
> *They will soar on wings like eagles; they will run and not grow*
> *weary, they will walk and not be faint.*
> (Isaiah 40:31)

> *I can do everything through him who gives me strength.*
> (Philippians 4:13)

> *Let us not become weary in doing good,*
> *for at the proper time we will reap a harvest*
> *if we do not give up.*
> (Galatians 6:9)

Casting all your care upon him; for he careth for you.

(1 Peter 5:7 KJV)

So do not throw away your confidence; it will be richly rewarded.
You need to persevere so that when you have done the will of God,
you will receive what he has promised.

(Hebrews 10:35–36)

If any of you lacks wisdom, he should ask God, who gives gener-
ously without finding fault, and it will be given to him.

(James 1:5)

APPENDIX
C

Red Flags

WHILE THERE IS A CONSIDERABLE RANGE in the time it takes different children to reach language milestones, there are delays that are serious enough to require a little extra help.

A professional evaluation is recommended if

- you have difficulty understanding your child's speech;

- others have difficulty understanding him;

- your child has difficulty understanding others;

- your child seems uncomfortable with his speech;

- others tease him about the way he talks; and/or

- his voice sounds hoarse or in any way very different from others his age.

Referrals for evaluations can be obtained from your pediatrician, your hospital's speech and hearing clinic, or a speech specialist in the public school system.

If you do suspect a problem, try to keep an even keel until the information is all in. Even if some type of early intervention is recommended, don't panic. In a couple years your child may be completely caught up with his peers—whether or not he receives speech and language services. There is considerable debate around the effectiveness of early intervention for non-disabled children with moderate speech delays. As specialist Grover Whitehurst asserts, "It can get them talking a lot faster, but after a couple years you can't tell the difference between kids who had early intervention and those who did not."[10]

APPENDIX
D

Rethinking TV

IF YOU WANT TO GROW A great reader, you may need to rethink the role of TV in your family's life.

Studies are beginning to show a link between toddler TV viewing and later attention deficits in school.[11] The American Academy of Pediatrics describes the problem:

> Children in the United States watch about 4 hours of TV every day. Watching movies on tape and playing video games only adds to time spent in front of the TV screen. It may be tempting to use television, movies, and video games to keep your child busy, but your child needs to spend as much time growing and learning as possible. Playing, reading, and spending time with friends and family are much healthier than sitting in front of a TV screen.[12]

Not only is this a waste of time and threat to potential learning ability, but the overuse of TV with children can lead to obesity, as well as exposure to violence, sex, alcohol and drugs, and unnecessary commercialism.

The AAP warns:

> Children of all ages are constantly learning new things. The first
> 2 years of life are especially important in the growth and develop-
> ment of your child's brain. During this time, children need good,
> positive interaction with other children and adults. Too much tele-
> vision can negatively affect early brain development. This is espe-
> cially true at younger ages, when learning to talk and play with
> others is so important.
>
> Until more research is done about the effects of TV on very young
> children, the American Academy of Pediatrics (AAP) does not rec-
> ommend television for children age 2 or younger. For older children,
> the Academy recommends no more than 1 to 2 hours per day of
> educational, nonviolent programs.[13]

How can you avoid relying on TV as babysitter? By getting your children more
involved with what you do. Instead of getting them out from under your feet while
you cook dinner, for instance, bring a stool into the kitchen and let them watch
you, thinking of ways to get them involved. As I discussed in *Mommy, Teach Me!*
spending quality time this way with Mom will do more for their self-esteem than
a year of Barney.

If your children are in the TV habit, it may be hard to break at first and they
may seem restless and at a loss for what to do with themselves. You can introduce
activities, but also give it some time. Kids are truly resourceful. If your home is
set up with places where they can entertain themselves—some hooks with dress-
up clothes, coloring books, building blocks, a basket of Duplos, shelves of picture
books—they will figure something out.

They will be the better for it. Some adults struggle all their lives with their own
tendency to be couch potatoes. Why set your kids up for that kind of failure?

With your desire for your child to have the best possible chance to reach his learning potential, be sure not to sabotage all your efforts with too much TV.

The AAP Web site has some good ideas for taming TV: http://www.aap.org/family/tv1.htm

✳ ✳ ✳

One alternative to television I *heartily* recommend is the Odyssey audio series produced by Focus on the Family. These programs are available on CD or audio-cassettes from Focus on the Family www.family.org/resources or 800-232-6459.

The series is chock-full of highly entertaining, thought-provoking stories with rich vocabulary and historical references. My children have listened to the tapes over and over.

Audio programs offer this distinct advantage: while television shows promote passivity, radio or tape programs encourage the child's brain to become actively engaged in creating the story as the child's imagination is required to supply the "visual."

APPENDIX
E

Where to Find Books

Amazon

They call themselves the World's Largest Bookstore—and you don't have to step outside your door to browse. For those on the Internet, this is an efficient way to buy books—when you know what you want. Search by title or author, find discounted price, and add to your cyber shopping cart. I have never failed to find a book listed here. And be sure to check out the used editions of books you want—which often go for pennies. (www.amazon.com)

Christian Book Distributors

The Christian version of Amazon, often with competitive pricing—but without the used book feature. Visit www.christianbooks.com to order online or call 1-800-247-4784 for catalog.

Scholastic Book Clubs

A monthly offering of books, some at deep discounts. Set up as class handouts for different grade levels. Visit www.scholastic.com or call 1-800-724-6527 for teacher's catalog, share brochures with friends, then place an order together. But be forewarned: though you may find great prices on good books, you will need to weed through a lot of children's book garbage.

God's World Book Club

Operates just like Scholastic, only selection of books is more traditional and Christian. Visit www.gwbc.com or call 1-800-951-2665 for catalog.

Stuttering

MOST EXPERTS AGREE THAT A STUTTER that settles in to become a disability is caused by the parent's overreaction to it. Stuttering runs in families because a parent who stutters is even more worried than one who doesn't when he hears it in his own child. A parent who is overly conscious of his child's speech will often create the problem he wants so desperately to prevent. In speech, easy does it usually works best.

HOW TO STYMIE A STUTTER

- Listen to what your child is saying rather than to how he is saying it.
- Don't rush him.
- Don't finish his sentences.
- Don't tell him to slow down or to stop.
- Don't worry yourself nor pressure him.
- Act as though the stutter is not there.
- Share these guidelines with everyone close to your child.
- Relax.

If after six weeks of this minimizing policy your child's speech has not begun to return to normal, ask your pediatrician for a referral to a speech therapist.

Make Your Own Sandpaper Letters

(Only if you want to! Or buy substitutes from resources listed at 🍎 .)

You will need extra-thick and heavy posterboard, or something similar, cut into 5 x 7 inch rectangles.

Paint or cover the board with pink contact paper for consonants, blue for vowels.

Using templates available at 🍎 , cut letters (remember: only lowercase) from fine sandpaper.

Use rubber cement to glue sandpaper letters onto board, being careful to align the letter 3/4 inch from the right side of the rectangle. This placement leaves an empty space on the left where the child will place his left hand while tracing the letter with his right (just as we steady a piece of paper with one hand while writing with another).

Place a red dot on each letter to remind your child where to begin tracing (see appendix H—correct letter formation).

Note: You can purchase a very adequate set of small sandpaper letters (4 1/4 x 2 5/8 inch)—pink for consonants and blue for vowels—from www.didax.com for $19.95.

Correct Letter Formation

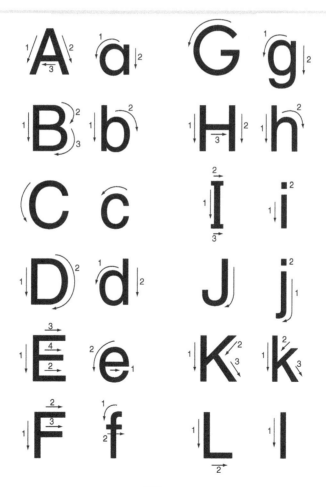

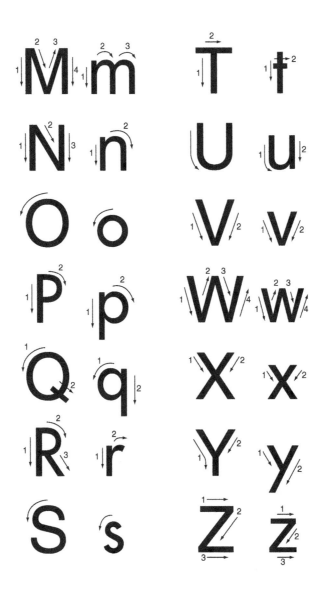

Lefties Need a Little More Thought

AS A RIGHT-HANDED PARENT OF ELEVEN right-handed children, until we adopted our twelfth—who turned out to be a lefty—I had not much considered the issue of handedness. Fortunately, while writing *Ready, Set, Read!* I had done a little digging to address the concerns of parents of lefties.

When my library research turned up nothing significant, I went to the Internet, found the newsgroup for lefties (alt.lefthanders) and asked the real experts—lefties themselves (some 10 to 13 percent of the population)—for input. I received many replies, some detailing real horror stories of what they had endured as children because of adults intent on changing their left-handed orientation. These included physical punishment as well as humiliation and isolation within the classroom. These stories, coupled with the fact that these children still grew up to be left-handed adults, certainly offer convincing evidence that God did indeed make some people left-handed.

So, if you have encouraged your child to grasp with his right hand by handing him rattles and spoons toward his right, yet he still consistently prefers his left, don't fight it. Accept the fact that you have a lefty. If you are left-handed yourself, though you will already know much about how to teach him, you may still benefit from some of the following suggestions. If you are right-handed, you will definitely need a crash course in translating the learning-to-write process for your child.

To teach a lefty, a left-handed parent should sit to the right and model the left-handed position. Many on the Internet felt that their own right-handed parents and teachers had been most effective when seated across from them in a mirror position. One man said that in spite of many lessons at shoe tying, he never "got it" until he happened to come into the room when his mother was tying her own shoes. Fascinated, he watched (as in the "mirror position"), then was finally able to repeat the process on his own shoes.

The best writing position for a lefty is the reverse of that for a right-handed person: the paper should be tilted to the right, with the bottom right-hand corner angled toward the chest. Encourage your child to hold the pencil so that his hand is not curving up over the top (although some lefties do this, many resist this tendency to avoid smearing their writing). The immediate problem then becomes how to anchor the paper. Since we write left to right, if the right hand anchors the paper on the right side, it will be in the way of the writing. The solution seems to be to bring the right arm over the top of the paper and anchor the top left corner with the right hand.

There is more involved to complicate the writing process for lefties: our letters are really formed with a left-to-right orientation. None of the online lefties who responded were completely happy with their handwriting. Some had opted for printing, especially all capitals. In teaching left-handed children to write, avoid holding a standard for them that they cannot achieve. Avoid clinging rigidly to the "correct" letter formation process—it may just be too difficult for a left-handed child to write a certain letter the way we teach it. For example, insisting that *t*'s be crossed from left to right creates more difficulty for a left-handed child. This is one area where the results—consistently readable handwriting and hopefully enjoyment of the writing process—are more important than the details of the process.

I was also advised by lefties to ask parents to advocate for their left-handed children when they go to school: three-ring binders are out for lefties. Spiral note-books are as well, unless the teacher can agree to let them write on the back of the pages as though they were the front.

Helps

My Favorite Workbooks

Merrill Phonics Skilltext Series—for phonetic skills, verb tenses, plurals, alphabetizing, etc.

Level R—reading readiness

Level A—beginning readers

Levels B–F as child progresses

Merrill Reading Skilltext—for reading comprehension, study skills, etc.

Going Places—reading readiness

Bibs, Mack, Joy—in sequence for beginning readers

To order, visit www.sraonline.com or call 1-888-SRA-4543.

Teaching Supply Sources

School Specialty (www.schoolspecialty.net)

A comprehensive site offering everything in the way of classroom supplies, from tables and chairs to rhythm instruments to early childhood manipulatives. Catalog available on request.

Discount School Supply (www.discountschoolsupply.com)

Extensive selection—more than enough for the needs of a family—and discount prices!

Classroom Direct (www.classroomdirect.com)

This site claims to have the lowest prices and offers free shipping for orders totaling more than $49.

BIBLIOGRAPHY

These were books I used to research and validate my own experience and observations of the language development/reading process.

Beadle, Muriel. *A Child's Mind: How Children Learn During the Critical Years from Birth to Age Five.* Garden City, New York: Doubleday and Company, 1970.

Gould, Toni S. *Get Ready to Read: A Practical Guide for Teaching Young Children at Home and in School.* New York: Walker & Co, 1991.

Lattman, Michelle, and Antoinette Seandel. *Better Speech for Your Child.* New York: Weyden Books, 1977.

Warner, Silas, MD, and Edward B. Rosenberg. *Your Child Learns Naturally: What Can You Do to Help Prepare Your Child for School?* Garden City, New York: Doubleday and Company, 1976.

Weiner, Harvey S. *Talk with Your Child: How to Develop Reading and Language Skills through Conversation at Home.* New York: Viking, 1988.

Contacting Barbara Curtis

Barbara speaks at MOPS (Mothers of Preschoolers) meetings,
women's retreats, and homeschool and writer's conferences.
Please visit her Web site www.barbaracurtis.com
or blog www.MommyLife.net.

Notes

[1] "Declining Literacy Skills," *Las Vegas Review and Journal*, March 2, 2006, http://www.reviewjournal.com/lvrj_home/2006/Mar-02-Thu-2006/news/6125447.html (accessed 8/22/06).

[2] The story of how I became a Christian and how God put all the pieces of my life together is available at my Web site, www.barbaracurtis.com or on my blog www.mommylife.net.

[3] C. S. Lewis, "Sometimes Fairy Stories May Say Best What's to Be Said," *On Stories: and Other Essays on Literature.* (Fort Washington, PA: Harvest Books, 1982), 48.

[4] Toni S. Gould, *Get Ready to Read: A Practical Guide for Teaching Young Children at Home and in School* (New York: Walker & Co, 1991), 33.

[5] Down syndrome is a condition in one out of eight hundred children in which an extra chromosome is found on the twenty-first pair (hence the medical name Trisomy 21). Though limited in intelligence, these children—especially when raised in loving, supportive homes—can grow to be actively contributing members of society, with their own unique gifts to offer. As the mother of four sons with Down syndrome (one by birth and three by adoption), I know emphatically that

Down syndrome is not an unhappy ending, just the beginning of a different kind of story.

[6] I use the term *differently-abled* rather than *disabled* not out of any reactionary political correctness but because it seems the most accurate way to reflect how we appear in God's eyes. Fanny Cosby, a great hymn writer who was blind from infancy, did not "see" with her physical eyes the way we do, yet she could "see" things in the spiritual realm few are privileged to see.

[7] C. S. Lewis quote, "The Weight of Glory" (San Francisco: HarperCollins, 2001), 140.

[8] Anna Mulrine, "Losing Our History," *U.S. News & World Report,* November 19, 2003, 68.

[9] Ibid.

[10] George Whitehurst, "need name of article", *Newsweek,* Spring 1997, 23. This was in a special *Newsweek* issue on child development.

[11] Dimitri A. Christakis, MD. "Early Television Exposure and Subsequent Attentional Problems in Children," *Pediatrics* (http://pediatrics.aappublications. org/cgi/content/abstract/113/4/708).

[12] Need author of article, "Television and the Family," *American Academy of Pediatrics* (www.aap.org/family/tv1.htm).

[13] Ibid.

Notes

Notes

Notes

Notes

Notes

Notes

Notes

Notes

Notes

Notes